PRAISE FOR *REAL CONFIDENCE*

"Simone's words are a refreshing reminder that confidence begins with self-respect. Her stories are honest, human, and exactly what women need right now."

Tina Wells, Founder, Entrepreneur, and Author

"We don't talk enough about the invisible wounds—the ones that live quietly beneath the surface of success. Simone Knego does. She reminds us that healing doesn't begin when the pain ends—it begins when you choose yourself. *REAL Confidence* is both a mirror and a map for every woman ready to stop abandoning herself and start honoring her own strength."

Gia Lacqua, Chief Empowerment Officer of Elevate and author of *PowerShift*

"This book made me stop and really think about how I talk to myself, and honestly, I realized I was way more critical than I ever knew. Simone's stories are so relatable; one minute you're laughing, the next you're tearing up. Her insights and practical frameworks make it feel possible to shift the way you think about yourself and build real, doable confidence."

Lena B. Taylor, Founder of Flipping Gorgeous

"With vulnerability and authenticity, Simone shares the necessary components for real, lasting confidence. She weaves in relatable stories, and she provides useful strategies that are easy to remember and implement. The psychologist in me appreciates how she connects her ideas to the research."

Dr. Peggy DeLong, The Gratitude Psychologist and Founder of Midlife Awakening Sisterhood

"Loved *REAL Confidence* by Simone Knego. It's honest, raw, and so relatable. A beautiful reminder that confidence isn't about perfection—it's about showing up for yourself, even on the hard days."

Sally Harris, Coach for Estranged Moms

"Simone doesn't just talk about confidence—she shows you how to build it, one honest step at a time. This book is raw, real, and exactly the reminder we all need that self-doubt doesn't define us, but our choices do."

AJ Vaden, CEO and Co-Founder of Brand Builders Group, *New York Times* bestselling author of *Wealthy and Well-Known*

"Simone's book shows women that confidence doesn't come from perfection; it comes from presence. The messages she shares are both transformational and deeply empowering."

Jessica Papineau, CEO/Founder of CSJ Styling

"Poignant stories and actionable tips to gain REAL Confidence. What every midlife woman (or any woman) starting a new story or going through reinvention needs. Simone's book reads like an insightful conversation with a supportive BFF. Inspiration gold!"

Kim Costa, Author and TV Host, "American Dream TV"

"*Real Confidence* is an honest, heartfelt look at what it means to believe in yourself—especially when it doesn't come easily. Simone encourages women to quiet their inner critic and speak to themselves with more kindness. I especially loved the "Embrace Your Failures" section—such a great reminder that confidence often grows out of the moments we learn the most about ourselves."

Stacy Harris, Networking Strategist

"*Real Confidence* is a beautiful blend of relatable stories, practical tools, and heartfelt wisdom. Simone writes with such courage and authenticity that you can't help but see yourself in her journey. Her framework and exercises create a clear path toward building confidence that lasts, reminding us that if she can do it, we can too."

Whitney Faires, Speaker, Leadership Advisor, and Executive Coach

"From the opening line, I felt both seen and at peace. Simone's genuine voice is refreshingly authentic—like a reassuring presence reminding you that you're not alone and that you deserve to feel confident."

Courtney Youngs, Author of *The Waggle Dance* & Corporate Communicator

"No matter where you are in life, this book will remind you of your inner power. It will ignite the confidence that we all get to cultivate in this lifetime. A must-read for any woman who is ready to get real with themselves so they can build the life they truly want."

Gabrielle Scout Maio, Founder of Scout's Agency

"This book feels like a conversation with a wise friend who reminds you to give yourself grace while still cheering you forward. It's heartfelt, honest, and beautifully human. As someone who coaches leaders to lead with heart, I love how Simone leads her readers with vulnerability and courage. Her message hits home, personally and professionally. It's a MUST read for all!"

Jaime Marco, Creator of UnFunkt™, Keynote Speaker, Leadership & Connection Catalyst

"*REAL Confidence* hit me in a way I didn't expect. There were so many moments where I felt like Simone was putting words to things I've felt but never said out loud. It's not one of those surface-level self-help books—it's real, it's raw, and it meets you right where you're at. It reminded me a lot of what I try to live and teach through XYL—that confidence isn't something you're born with; it's something you build, one small act of courage at a time. It just made me stop, reflect, and remember what it means to show up for yourself—even when it's hard."

Kelsey Lensman, Founder of Xpand Your Limits

"From the very first words, Simone drew me in with her captivating and raw storytelling. *REAL Confidence* is a powerful tool for encouraging readers to own their stories, prioritize true self-care, and pursue their dreams with courage and clarity."

Shannon Acheson, Author of *Home Made Lovely* and *The Clutter Fix.*

"Simone, your words didn't just resonate with me, they anchored me. When you wrote, 'Confidence doesn't come from getting everything right. It comes from rising after you fall and choosing to trust the woman who stands back up,' I felt something in my spirit settle. For so long, I believed confidence meant being flawless, executing perfectly, leading without wavering, showing strength without letting the broken pieces show. But life has a way of reminding us that true strength isn't polished… it's persevering."

Susan Semmelmann, CEO/Founder of Semmelmann Interiors

"I am privileged to know Simone personally, and she is the real deal—authentic, wise, and generous in how she shares what she's learned. This book reflects the same integrity and insight she brings to her life and work every day, offering a grounded, deeply practical path to leading with confidence and purpose."

Shayna Kreisler, Vice President, Lay Leadership Development,
The Jewish Federations of North America

"If you've ever felt uncertain about your life's journey, *REAL Confidence* is the guide you've been waiting for. Simone is the trusted mentor and friend who shows us that courage isn't something we're born with—it's something we build, one brave, honest step at a time. I can't wait for women everywhere to read this book."

Allison Trowbridge, Author & Founder/CEO of Copper Books

REAL CONFIDENCE

REAL CONFIDENCE

A Simple Guide to Go from Unsure to Unshakeable

Simone Knego

Real Confidence: A Simple Guide to Go from Unsure to Unshakeable

Published by Copper Books, Nashville, Tennessee.

Distributed by Simon & Schuster.

Printed in the United States of America.
First edition 2026.

Front cover design by Sami Lane.
Layout and jacket design by George Stevens, G Sharp Design, LLC.

ISBN 979-8-9912674-9-6 (hardcover)
ISBN 979-8-9912674-3-4 (eBook)

Library of Congress Control Number: 2025926418

For my daughters, Emma, Olivia, and Mili.

Watching you grow into the women you are becoming is the greatest honor of my life. May you always believe in yourselves the way I believe in you.

Scan to access the reader guide, exercises, and other supporting resources.

realconfidencebook.com
/resources

CONTENTS

AUTHOR'S NOTE

Throughout this book you'll encounter various thought-provoking prompts, exercises, and questions. These were developed to help you further examine and process the lessons contained within these pages. They're not there as tasks to complete but as invitations to pause, explore, and grow. Before embarking on your journey to gain REAL confidence, take a moment to gather a few simple materials:

1. A journal or notebook
2. A pen or pencil
3. A sheet of paper and/or a colorful sheet of paper

You don't need these materials to read the book, but having them ready will help you turn awareness into action. Think of them as companions on this journey, ready to capture your breakthroughs, realizations, and moments of truth.

INTRODUCTION

I thought I knew what I was doing.

I had already raised three children. I'd navigated sleepless nights, tantrums, and teething. So, when my husband and I adopted our son, Noah, from South Korea, I thought I'd be ready. While my husband stayed home with our two daughters, Emma and Olivia, I boarded a plane with our son Jacob and flew across the ocean to bring Noah home. I carried hope, joy, and excitement with me—and just a touch of nervousness too. But nothing about that trip, or that transition, went the way I imagined.

From the moment we boarded the plane for the long flight home, Noah cried. No, that's not right. He *screamed.* The kind of high-pitched, relentless cry that makes your heart race and your palms sweat.

I bounced him. I whispered. I walked up and down the aisle. Nothing helped.

Eventually, I ended up in the galley … standing for hours, rocking him while flight attendants shuffled around me and passengers peeked behind the curtain, trying to catch a glimpse of the woman who couldn't quiet her baby.

I kept saying, "I'm so sorry. I'm doing my best." But inside, my thoughts were spinning.

Why can't I do this? What kind of mother am I? What if I'm not enough for him?

I had spent extra money to upgrade to first class, thinking we'd get more space to rest, maybe even sleep. In my mind, we'd recline our seats, he'd fall asleep on my chest, and we'd wake up halfway home.

But real life doesn't follow the picture-perfect version we create in our heads.

Noah wouldn't sleep. He didn't want the bassinet. He didn't want me to hold him. He didn't want anyone.

The stares from our fellow passengers were relentless. Some looked annoyed. Some pitied me. A few were kind. But most just wanted me, and my screaming baby, *out of their bubble.*

At one point, a flight attendant gently asked, "Can I try the Korean way?"

I would've handed her Noah *and* the keys to my house if it meant he'd stop crying.

She slung him onto her back, hunched over, and began bouncing at a ninety-degree angle. Two minutes later—silence. He was asleep. I stared in disbelief.

Whatever magic she used, it worked. I was so grateful I could've cried.

That entire trip stripped me down to my core. I was exhausted, holding on by a thread, and trying to comfort a baby who didn't want to be comforted by me. Every cry felt like proof that I was failing. Every stare from the people around me pressed in just a little harder. I had pictured it so differently. I thought

I'd bring home our son and ease him into our family with love and patience. Instead, I felt helpless, raw, and unsure if I was getting any of it right.

We landed back in Sarasota after delayed flights, an unexpected overnight in Chicago, and more tears than I could count. By the time I finally made it to the luggage carousel and saw my husband, Rob, waiting for us, I was completely spent. He was standing there with our daughters and a group of friends holding "Welcome Home" signs. They were smiling, waving, laughing. It was a celebration. But the second I locked eyes with Rob, everything I had been holding in came rushing out and I broke down. I handed Noah to him, buried my face in his chest, and sobbed. I was emotionally wrecked. I needed someone else to carry the weight for a minute. And in that moment, Rob held both of us, me and Noah, in his arms.

One of our funniest family photos was taken right there at the airport. You can see Noah mid-scream, our eight-year-old daughter, Emma, with her hands clamped over her ears, and me with eyes so swollen I look like I lost a boxing match. It's the kind of photo that perfectly says, "Welcome home! We survived … barely."

By the time we got home, I had nothing left in the tank. I went straight to the bathroom, shut the door, and collapsed on the cold tile floor.

I cried until I couldn't breathe.

Cried from exhaustion.

From shame.

From fear that I wasn't strong enough for this life I had chosen.

I had been a mother for over a decade, and yet in that moment, I felt like I knew nothing.

And that wasn't the first time I found myself questioning everything. I've been on the bathroom floor more times than I can count. I've cried from heartbreak, exhaustion, fear, and the weight of trying to hold everything together. I've been there after abuse—completely broken, unsure if I could ever feel whole again. I've been there in motherhood—overwhelmed and doubting whether I was getting anything right. I've been there as a working mom trying to do everything—juggling the needs, the schedules, the responsibilities—while putting myself last.

Maybe your version looks different, but I wonder if you've felt that same kind of unraveling. The kind of pressure that makes you question your worth, your strength, and if you're doing any of it right.

Today I'm a mom of six, three biological children and three adopted. My life has been full, beautiful, and messy, and many days it's been a struggle. If your life feels full, beautiful, and messy too—especially if it doesn't look the way you imagined—you're not alone. I've lived through moments that stopped me in my tracks. Moments when I've caught my reflection and thought, *I don't even recognize myself anymore.* Because no matter how much I've done or how far I've come, I've had to wrestle with something so many of us carry: self-doubt.

If you've ever felt like you're failing at something you thought you should be good at … If you've ever questioned your strength, your purpose, or whether you're even allowed to want more … If you've ever felt like you've lost sight of who you really are—this book is for you.

This isn't a highlight reel. It's an honest, in-depth look at what it really takes to build confidence from the inside out—whether yours has been shaken, shattered, or something you've struggled to feel at all.

I didn't find my way *back* to myself; I *found myself*—through the hard moments, the broken ones, and the brave ones. I did it by using what I now call **The REAL Method™**, a framework that helped me rebuild my confidence from the inside out.

That's what I want to share with you in these pages: the real stories, the honest struggle, and the method that helped me rise—not into perfection, but into a version of myself that I respect, love, and finally believe in.

Confidence doesn't come from getting everything right. It comes from rising after you fall and choosing to trust the woman who stands back up.

I see you. I know you've had moments when you doubted everything you thought you knew. Moments when you questioned everything about yourself. Moments when you wondered if wanting more made you selfish. That kind of doubt can feel heavy, but it doesn't define you. I wrote this book to show you that REAL confidence isn't something you're born with. It's something you can build, step by step, in your own way and in your own time.

You don't have to have it all figured out. You don't have to be fearless. What matters is that you're willing to take the next step toward yourself. And I'll be right here, walking with you.

By the end, you'll have a clearer sense of who you are and what you're made of. You're going to find your mountain moment. Now let me tell you about mine.

Chapter One

LET'S GET REAL!

"If you're always trying to be normal, you will never know how amazing you can be."[1]

MAYA ANGELOU

There I stood, 8,000 miles from home at the base of Mount Kilimanjaro, deep in the Tanzanian rainforest. The summit stretched 19,341 feet into the sky, the tallest free-standing mountain in the world. To put that in perspective, that's taller than fourteen Empire State Buildings stacked on top of each other. It didn't just look big. It looked impossible. And as I tilted my head back to take it all in, a mix of awe and panic washed over me.

I wasn't climbing alone. There were sixteen of us, teammates who had been complete strangers just a week earlier. I had trained for six months to make this climb. I had said yes. I had prepared. I had packed. Still, no amount of training prepares you for the moment you're actually there, standing at the base of something that suddenly feels much bigger than you imagined.

What was I thinking when I agreed to this?

ME—the self-proclaimed couch athlete who literally needs to book a session with a personal trainer just to make it to the gym.

ME—the mother of six, who had never climbed anything taller than a Florida overpass.

And yet somehow, I signed up thinking, *Yeah, sure. Let's do that.*

Oh, and did I mention the bathroom situation? Because here's what no one tells you when you decide to climb a giant mountain: nature doesn't come with plumbing. DUH. And squatting behind a rock in subzero temperatures is … not ideal.

So, I brought a Shewee. Yes, it's exactly what it sounds like—a pee funnel that lets you stand and go without freezing your butt off. Weird? Absolutely. Messy? Shockingly, no. And I have to admit, peeing standing up and writing my name in the snow felt pretty badass. Honestly, it was one of the most unexpectedly empowering moments of the trip. If I could pee through a funnel, in freezing temps, without splashing my boots, I could pretty much conquer the world. Who knew a pee funnel could make you feel so powerful?

Still, even with my newly discovered snow-writing skills, the doubt crept in. I had trained. I had packed. I had said yes. But standing there, staring up at the summit, I continued to question everything.

What was I thinking?

I mean, I call walking the dog cardio, and here I was standing at the base of a mountain that looked like it should come with a warning label. But I had made a promise to myself and to others.

I was climbing to raise money for the Livestrong Foundation, and I wasn't about to let fear (or frostbite) win.

So, I focused on my *why*. I tightened my laces, grabbed my walking sticks, and took the first step.

And then the next.

And then the next.

FINDING MY OWN UNSHAKEABLE CONFIDENCE

On the fifth day of our climb, we began the final ascent at 11:00 p.m. and hiked through the darkness of night. I was mentally and physically exhausted, but adrenaline kept me moving. The voice of doubt, aka the What-if Whisperer, had followed me from the start. At 5,000 feet I kept going. At 10,000 feet I kept going. At 15,000 feet I kept going. But as we began the final stretch in the freezing darkness, the What-if Whisperer came roaring back. But she wasn't a whisper anymore. She was loud. Relentless.

Who do you think you are?

You're too old for this.

You're not fit enough. Not strong enough. Not mentally tough enough.

Why did you ever think you could do this?

With one negative thought chasing the next, I kept going. Slowly. Deliberately. Methodically. My headlamp lit a narrow circle in front of me as we climbed in silence, switchback after switchback, winding higher into the night. Every step was intentional. Every breath felt like a battle.

The voice in my head kept circling back:

Can I do this? Can I finish what I started?

You're forty-two years old. You're NOT a climber. You have six kids at home. What are you thinking?

But I didn't stop.

I kept putting one foot in front of the other.

I was out of breath, my body hurt to the core, and my knee had swollen into a balloon. Just as the sun began to rise, casting light across the snow and peaks around us, I pushed through one last switchback. I looked up and the horizon seemed to go on forever. I was standing at the top of Mount Kilimanjaro.

The sky was an unbelievable shade of blue. The ground was covered in bright white snow mixed with dirt from the boots that had walked the path before me. And then, on a weathered brown wooden sign that had clearly seen better days, were the words I had been longing to see—the ones the relentless voice in my head swore I never would:

CONGRATULATIONS! You are now at UHURU Peak, Tanzania. Africa's highest point.

I pulled out my phone to snap a photo of the view—snow-covered peaks, sunlight streaking across the sky, the world stretching out beneath me. It took my breath away.

And then I saw it. Three bars. I had *three bars*. Impossible. I didn't even stop to think—I hit "call." And when my husband answered, I couldn't hold it in. The second I heard his voice, the tears came. Hot tears against freezing air, sliding down my cheeks and instantly turning cold. They didn't stop. *I* couldn't stop.

I was standing at the highest point in Africa, sobbing into the phone, trying to get words out through a cracked voice and frozen lips. The connection was spotty, the air thin, and I could barely breathe. Then I heard it—my family on the other end. The kids were cheering like I'd just won the Super Bowl, which of course made the dogs lose their minds. Suddenly there was barking, then more cheering, then the kids yelling at the dogs to stop barking and then yelling at each other to stop yelling. Within seconds, the whole house was in full-blown chaos.

Even from 19,000 feet up, the beautiful madness of my house had found me. And that's when it hit me: This was why I was here. Not to escape the noise, but to remind myself what I'm capable of. To step out of my comfort zone, to rise above my fears, and to prove to myself that I could do something I never thought I could do.

As I struggled to suck air into my oxygen-deprived lungs, I did a little celebration dance—at least inside my head. My body wasn't moving. It was too busy trying to breathe. But still, that invisible happy dance was enough to quiet the What-if Whisperer inside my head. Not because she disappeared, but because I was finally following through.

I did the things I said I would. I kept showing up—for myself. And in that consistency, the doubt lost its grip.

That changed everything.

"I did IT."

"I DID it."

"IIIII did it."

For the first time in my life, at forty-two years old, I realized what it felt like to believe in myself. And with that, I finally understood what it meant to see my own value and to feel like I was worthy of my own respect.

And here's why I'm sharing this with you: I don't tell this story so you'll be impressed that I climbed a mountain. I tell it because I want you to see that confidence isn't about Kilimanjaro at all. It's about showing up for yourself, step after step, even when doubt is screaming at you. It's proof of what you're capable of when you refuse to stop, even when the mountain in front of you feels too steep.

IT'S UP TO US TO SHATTER OUR SELF-DOUBT

When I reflect on my Mount Kilimanjaro experience—the thoughts, the doubts, the limiting beliefs, the mean things I said to myself—I remind myself that through it all, I kept going.

By putting one foot in front of the other, I was honoring myself. I was keeping the commitments I had made to myself. I was respecting myself.

Confidence might *begin* with that first step, but it's *built* in the next one. The one you take when it's hard. When no one's watching. That's the step that counts.

By staying connected to my why and putting one foot in front of the other, something started to shift. With each step, my confidence grew—not in some dramatic, overnight way, but steadily and with effort. By the time I reached the summit, something in me had shifted forever.

Confidence might *begin* with that first step, but it's *built* in the next one.

I brought a new kind of understanding down the mountain with me; an understanding that I was capable of far more than I had ever allowed myself to believe.

What I've come to realize is that climbing Mount Kilimanjaro is no different than asking for a raise, sharing your ideas in a boardroom, or applying for a job that seems beyond your reach. Climbing Kilimanjaro was me—yes, ME—saying yes to a version of myself that I didn't even know existed yet.

What about YOU? Have you ever said no to something you wanted to do because self-doubt stopped you from even trying? Turned down a project at work because you doubted your ability to succeed? Let someone dismiss your idea in a meeting because you didn't feel confident to stand up for yourself? Skipped applying for a job you really wanted because you thought you didn't meet every qualification? Stayed home from an event because you felt you wouldn't fit in?

Those are just a handful of ways that self-doubt can show up in our lives. I bet most of us have experienced some, or all, of these moments. And I'm certain *all* of us have experienced many other moments just like these. The truth is that self-doubt affects everyone, regardless of age, background, or generation. But here is the good news: The choices that got me to that summit are the same kinds of choices you can use to move past doubt and toward the life you want. So, if you struggle with self-doubt, rest assured that you're not alone.

Research shows how common this really is. Did you know that close to 80 percent of women struggle with low self-esteem and shy away from self-advocacy?[2] In other words, four out of five women are being negatively affected because of a lack of confidence.

According to a survey by Indeed, 97 percent of respondents believe confidence is important when seeking a promotion, and 94 percent believe it's a major contributor to career growth,[3] yet as women, we struggle across the board with self-doubt.

Self-doubt is one of the biggest things that can keep you from reaching your full potential. It keeps you stuck, questioning yourself, and afraid to take the next step. And the longer it lingers, the harder it becomes to move forward.

Self-doubt can make you overanalyze everything, leading to missed opportunities, low self-esteem, and stunted growth both personally and professionally. And what's more, self-doubt will follow you every moment of every day if you let it.

But there's good news. It might be hard for you to believe if you've let the What-if Whisperer run your life for a while, but it's still true: You have the power within you to take back control from your self-doubt, just like I did, and to achieve REAL confidence for yourself.

And I want to show you how.

LET'S GET R.E.A.L. WITH OURSELVES

Through my own personal journey and in working with hundreds of women who struggle with self-doubt, I've discovered that there's really only one solution to overcoming self-doubt and reaching your full potential: confidence.

I'm sure that's not mind-blowing to anyone, but it is 100 percent true.

What most people don't realize is that confidence is an inside job. It isn't something you're born with. It's not a fixed personality trait. And it's definitely not some elusive unicorn characteristic you either have or you don't.

Confidence is an inside job.

Confidence is built—step by step, choice by choice. It's a skill. And if you want to build it, you need to build it from the inside out. And let's be honest—you're going to want to build it because you need confidence to perform at your peak, both at work and in life in general.

So, how do you build confidence?

You build confidence through action, by following through on the commitments you make to yourself. You build it when you take the first step and then the next one after that. You build it by showing up when it's uncomfortable, and by facing your fears head-on, especially when no one else is watching.

After interviewing hundreds of women, I've realized that everyone defines confidence a little differently. To me, confidence means being fully yourself—being real—no matter who you're with or where you are. It's not about holding back to make others comfortable or pushing forward to prove something. It's about showing up as you are, without adding or editing parts of yourself to fit in.

Confidence isn't the absence of fear. It's about facing your fears and moving forward despite them. As Eleanor Roosevelt said, "Nothing has ever been achieved by the person who says, 'It can't be done.' Do the things you think you cannot do."[4]

But how do we do this?

Over the last ten years, I have devoted myself to studying this kind of transformation to boil it down to a simple and repeatable framework I can share with others.

I call this framework The REAL Method™, and it can help you build confidence from the inside out.

The REAL Method™ focuses on four key pillars for building confidence:

- RESPECT YOU-RSELF (yes, I write it like this on purpose)
- EMBRACE YOUR FAILURES
- ASK YOURSELF WHAT YOU WANT
- LIVE WITHOUT LIMITS

It's about building self-respect, self-acceptance, self-worth, and self-confidence. I've found that when we're willing to get REAL with ourselves, we can build REAL confidence in ourselves and help others to do the same.

In the following chapters, we're going to take a deep dive into the four individual pillars of The REAL Method™. We're going to talk about what each pillar means, how it works, and the work you need to do to create REAL confidence in your life.

If you're serious about kicking self-doubt to the curb once and for all, you're in the right place. So, sit back, buckle up, and read on. You're in for the ride of your life because things are about to get REAL.

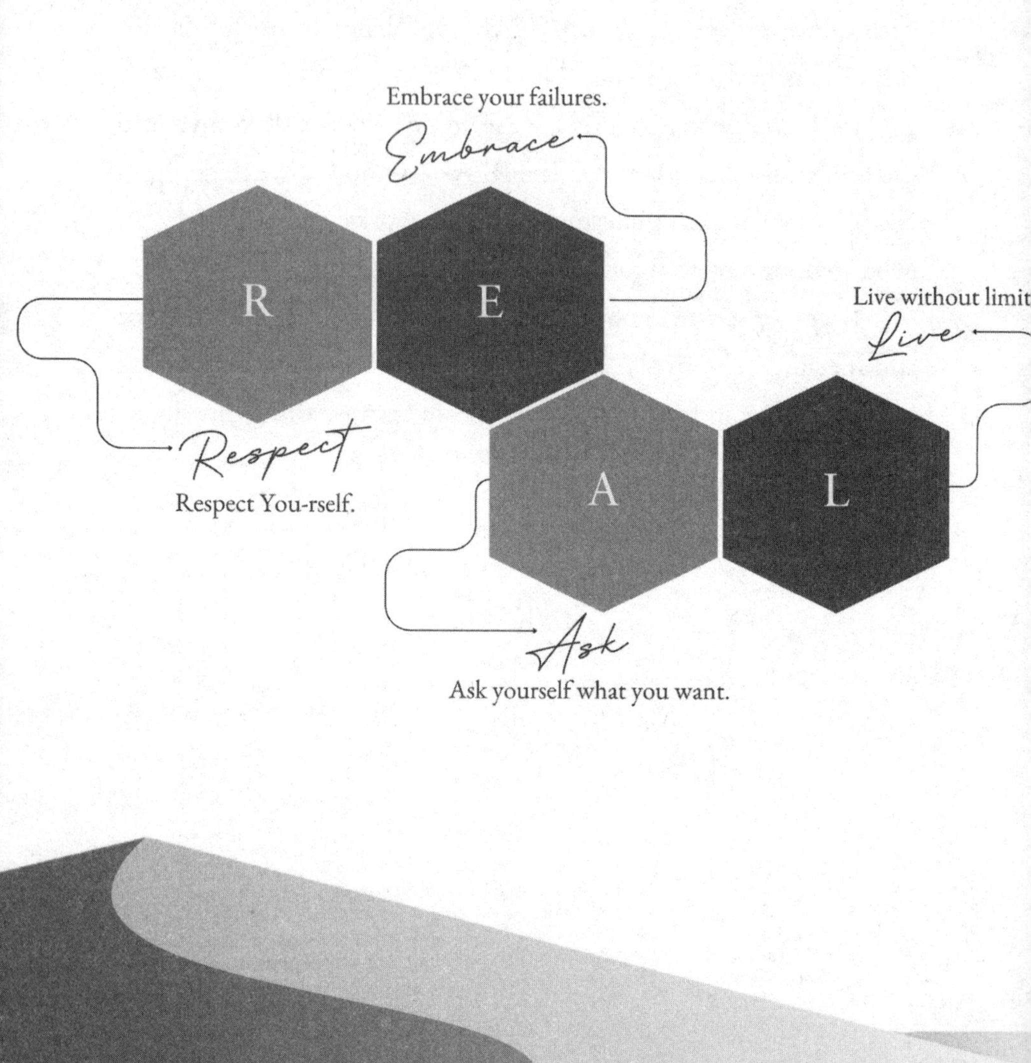
Embrace your failures.
Embrace
R
E
Live without limit
Live
Respect
Respect You-rself.
A
L
Ask
Ask yourself what you want.

PILLAR #1

RESPECT YOU-RSELF

Respecting yourself means valuing and appreciating yourself as you are. It involves acknowledging your worth, embracing your strengths and imperfections, and treating yourself with kindness and dignity. It's about maintaining a positive self-image, fostering self-compassion, and honoring your own needs and boundaries. In essence, it's seeing yourself with the same respect and care that you would offer to your best friend.

Chapter Two

OWN YOUR WORTH

"Respect yourself enough to walk away from anything that no longer serves you, grows you, or makes you happy."[5]

ROBERT TEW

It's hard not to think of Aretha Franklin and her iconic song "Respect,"[6] the anthem that transformed a simple plea into a declaration of equality and empowerment. It was more than music; it was a movement that reminded women their worth didn't come from anyone else's validation. Decades later, we've made progress, but for many of us that inner kind of respect, the kind that starts within and shapes how we show up in the world, still doesn't come easily. For me and countless others, the challenge began long before we even realized it.

I grew up in Buffalo, New York, but right before high school started, my parents moved us to Florida. Leaving behind my childhood home and the friends I'd known my whole life was incredibly hard.

In Florida, I felt out of place—like I'd been dropped into someone else's story. I missed New York constantly, and more than anything, I just wanted to go back to the life I knew.

Given everything I was going through at the time, I found a lot of comfort in riding horses. I'd been riding since I was four years old, so being in the saddle felt like home, like the one piece of my old life I could still hold on to. My parents knew I needed something steady in my life, something that felt safe, so they bought me a horse. I named him Hannibal, and I rode him every chance I got.

One day while riding, I met another girl, and we quickly became friends. She's the one who introduced me to my first serious boyfriend. Let's call him John.

I was just fifteen when I met John. He seemed sweet, and he was definitely handsome, with these striking blue eyes that completely pulled me in. I was still missing my old life and friends in New York, and I carried around an emptiness that I couldn't quite shake.

John's attention filled that space, at least for a while. Before I knew it, I was spending all my time with him. He bought me flowers, took me to dinner, and did all those things you would expect a good boyfriend to do.

His attention came at a time when I really needed to feel seen. Still, at fifteen, I was obviously very young and inexperienced when it came to relationships. John wasn't my first boyfriend, but he was my first *serious* boyfriend, and this was new territory for me.

At the beginning of our relationship, he just seemed like a really nice guy. But it didn't take long before things started to change. He became super controlling, telling me what to eat, where to go, and who to hang out with. I now view that relationship from the perspective of a parent and cringe every time I think about what I would do if my daughter were to date someone like him. John was my worst nightmare, and I still struggle with the aftereffects of the abuse I experienced while I was with him.

Once he lured me in with his kindness, the verbal abuse began . . . and it never stopped.

He started saying horrible things to me. Things like, "I can't believe how fat you are," or "Look at all those stretch marks—disgusting."

At dinner, he'd say, "You should be eating a salad. You're already too fat."

He told me I wasn't pretty enough, that I should wear more makeup.

He said I wasn't smart enough and that I needed him to make decisions for me.

He didn't like my friends, so he told me to stop spending time with them.

Bit by bit, word by word, he chipped away at my confidence until I couldn't find any left.

I can't even explain why, but every time he made a disparaging remark, I took it in.

I *listened* to him.

I let his words sink in like they were true, like he knew something about me that I didn't. The worst part was that I started believing him. He became the voice in my head and the measuring stick that I used to gauge my value. My self-worth was constantly based on what he said and the things he did.

I remember driving to his house because he hadn't been returning my calls. This was before cellphones, texting, instant messaging, or any of the million social media apps teenagers use today to reach someone. Back then, when someone didn't answer their home phone, you showed up at their door.

I pulled up just as he was walking out the front door, dressed in a tuxedo. A girl in a prom dress stood beside him, smiling. I got out of the car and ran toward him. "What's going on?" I asked, my voice shaking.

He didn't even pause.

He pushed me aside and got into the limo with her.

I stood there on the sidewalk, frozen. My chest felt tight, and my mind was racing.

Maybe I misunderstood. Maybe there's an explanation. Maybe if I wait …

I didn't want to believe what had just happened.

So, I walked inside.

And I waited—on his parents' couch—while he went to prom with another girl.

I sat there in silence, staring at the floor, replaying everything, convincing myself that somehow this could still make sense. I couldn't walk away. That is how bad things were for me.

When he walked through the door, he laughed. *Laughed* that I was still there. He looked at me like I was pathetic and said, "Grow up. She didn't mean anything." And for a second, I believed him.

Because believing him was easier than facing the truth. Because facing the truth would've meant admitting I didn't recognize myself anymore.

At the time, I didn't understand that I was abandoning my own self-respect; I was too focused on him, on trying to win him over, on proving I was enough. **This is a reminder:** When you're constantly chasing someone else's approval, it's easy to lose sight of your own value. The realization that I wasn't respecting myself didn't come until much later. But looking back, that's exactly what was missing.

When you're constantly chasing someone else's approval, it's easy to lose sight of your own value.

I DIDN'T UNDERSTAND WHAT RESPECT WAS

As our relationship continued, so did his horrible behavior toward me.

I worked a part-time job, and he would always ask me if he could borrow money from me. It wasn't really borrowing, though, because he never paid me back. And once I gave him the money, he would spend it on other girls.

It was a constant pattern in our relationship. He would say or do one thing after another to tear me down and chip away at my self-worth.

During that time, I didn't respect myself enough to even understand what was happening. And I certainly lacked any kind of confidence.

When you're in the middle of something unhealthy, it's often hard to name it. You can't heal what you don't see, and that's why awareness is the first step to change.

You can't heal what you don't see, and that's why awareness is the first step to change.

I never looked in the mirror and asked myself, *Simone, what are you doing?*

All I could think about was pleasing him and making sure that John liked me. But even if he said he loved me, I still had zero confidence because I knew it would just be a matter of time until I disappointed him again. At least that's how I saw it.

The thing I just couldn't wrap my head around was why he didn't like me.

I kept telling myself, *He liked me in the beginning. What changed? What did I do wrong?*

Getting John to like me—*really* like me again—became the thing I chased. It was my driving force.

People-pleasing is often mistaken for love, but it's really a survival strategy. When you abandon yourself to be accepted by someone else, you're handing over your power.

That need to be liked always came before my need to be respected. I prioritized pleasing him over honoring myself, every single time. Still, he made me cry almost every day—because of the things he did, the things he said.

For three years, I lived in this exhausting cycle of trying to win him over and being broken down again and again. And then, the words turned into something worse. Two months after the prom incident, I found myself in the same place again, waiting at his house while he was out with another girl.

I sat there for hours, playing out conversations in my head, hoping this time would be different. That maybe he'd come home with an apology, or at least an explanation. When he finally walked through the door, it was late. He was drunk—stumbling, slurring his words.

I stood up and tried to talk to him, to tell him how much it hurt to always be treated like I didn't matter.

But instead of listening, or even looking at me, he swung.

He punched me in the face.

Just like that. No warning. No hesitation.

The pain was sharp, but what stayed with me more than the black eye was the shock. The silence after.

I didn't scream. I didn't run. I just stood there, holding my face, trying to process what had just happened.

His best friend came over and told me that I needed to walk away, but I couldn't. The next morning, he apologized and told me how much he loved me. I believed him.

Our relationship continued, and after eleventh grade, I left high school and started at Auburn University on early admission.

John followed me there but not because he had a plan or a future in mind. He followed me because he had nothing else.

He wasn't enrolled in school. He had no job, no money of his own (except what I gave him). At first, he rented a trailer in the middle of a field. I paid for most of it. Looking back, I can see it so clearly: I was his safety net, not his partner. He needed someone to survive off of, and I made myself that someone.

Sadly, the emotional and sometimes physical abuse didn't stop.

Fortunately, I had a little distance. I was living in a dorm, and I tried to stay there as much as I could. It wasn't full separation, but it gave me moments of space—moments where I could breathe, think, and begin to remember who I was without him.

In the one year I lived in Alabama, John moved three different times—always staying close, always trying to control everything I did. He was eventually hired at a bar and spent countless nights with other women yet still insisted we were in a relationship. He wanted the freedom to do whatever he wanted while controlling my every move.

He followed me when I moved back to Florida after my year at Auburn, and it was like nothing had changed. We slipped right back into the same toxic patterns. I found myself, once again, waiting at his house while he was out with another girl.

But this time, something in me had changed.

When he walked through the door, I didn't hold back.

I told him I was done—that I was leaving.

Deciding to walk away doesn't always feel strong. It can feel terrifying, lonely, even uncertain—but it's still a powerful decision.

That's when he looked me straight in the eye and said, "I'm going to kill you."

Then he came at me in a rage—eyes wild, fists clenched.

Before I could react, his hands were around my neck, and he started to strangle me. Everything blurred. I couldn't breathe. I couldn't speak. All I could think was, *This is really happening. This might be it.*

He was drunk—drunk enough that when I kicked him and shoved with everything I had, he stumbled backward and fell. I ran, heart pounding, legs shaking, but before I made it out the door, I glanced back.

He was crawling around, mumbling, trying to find his keys. That's what gave me the window to get away. I ran. I got into my car with trembling hands and drove straight home, barely able to catch my breath.

When I got home, I locked the door behind me and went straight to the bathroom. I sat on the floor, completely falling apart. I was crying—loud, uncontrollable sobs—shaking from fear, from shock, from everything that had just happened.

Yet underneath all of it, there was this wave of relief.

I had gotten out. I was alive.

But I didn't feel safe yet. I didn't feel okay.

I just sat there, holding myself, trying to breathe, trying to believe that it was over.

That night, something in me shifted. Sitting on that bathroom floor, I knew … I couldn't live like that anymore. I finally let myself see the truth: I deserved better. So, I made the decision to walk away.

Self-respect isn't always loud. Sometimes it looks like sitting on a bathroom floor, realizing your life has to change, and choosing yourself for the first time.

Self-respect isn't always loud. Sometimes it looks like sitting on a bathroom floor, realizing your life has to change, and choosing yourself for the first time.

And more than that, I made a promise to myself: I would never go back.

But leaving didn't mean the damage disappeared. The black eye faded, but the scars never did; they lived on in the way I saw myself and the way I doubted my worth for years, even decades. Many years later, even after meeting, marrying, and starting a family with a wonderful man, those scars still surfaced. Time and again, one of my kids would come running up from behind and wrap their little hands around my neck in a playful hug. Every time, my breath would catch and my heart would race. I'd smile so I wouldn't scare them, but inside, my body was screaming. That's the thing about trauma: It doesn't know the difference between love and danger. It just remembers.

I was eighteen when I had that moment of decision on my bathroom floor. That night, to be honest, I hadn't really thought about the importance of respecting myself. But looking back now, that moment—walking away—was the first time

I truly honored my worth. That was the beginning of reclaiming my self-respect.

Walking away wasn't easy. John continued to follow me around and stalk me.

One day, about a month after I left him, as I was driving home from work, I glanced in my rearview mirror—and my stomach dropped.

It was his car. He was following me. My heart started racing. I gripped the wheel tighter and tried to keep my focus. I didn't think. I just drove. Straight home.

When I pulled into the driveway, I saw my dad outside in the garden, bent over, pulling weeds. Relief hit me like a wave. I slammed the car door, ran toward him, and choked out the words through tears:

"Please, just keep him away from me!"

My dad stood up slowly, dusted the dirt off his hands, and looked me in the eye, calm but ready. With his thick Israeli accent, he said, "Don't worry. He won't come near you again."

And then, we waited. Sure enough, John pulled into the driveway seconds later. My dad didn't flinch. He stepped forward—calm, steady—and said in that same low, accented voice, "If you ever come near my daughter again, I will kill you."

He didn't yell. He didn't need to. His presence said everything. John drove away. That was the last time I ever saw him. Though this was the end of a very toxic and dangerous relationship, it was just the beginning of a long road for me to learn how to build my confidence.

RESPECTING YOURSELF BUILDS CONFIDENCE

One of the hardest parts about my relationship with John is that I walked away with more than just physical scars. I struggled mentally for years after our relationship, and I never addressed it. I didn't talk about it with anyone. I just figured it was who I was, someone who always doubted myself and constantly compared myself to others. That's who I allowed John to convince me I was.

But I'm no longer that girl—because I finally broke my silence. And while I've chosen to speak out, I hold deep respect for the women who haven't … or who may never. Their strength isn't measured by whether they share their story. Survival, in any form, is strength.

Still, I truly believe that if we can, we should talk about our challenging experiences much more than we do. There is such a high rate of young teenage girls and college students being abused by their partners and stripped of their confidence.

I know my story is not unique. There are many women whose confidence has been broken because of the cruel words and actions of another.

Like me, many girls and women have found themselves in relationships or jobs where they spend most of their time pleasing the people around them. It's a damaging cycle to get into. This kind of mindset leads so many of us to stay in toxic relationships or dead-end jobs where we are not respected by others and where we don't even respect ourselves.

I am certain that, like me, many women adopted this mindset at a very young age because of the abuse they suffered at the hands of another. Studies show that a whopping 76 percent of teens report psychological or emotional abuse during relationships.[7] That is a huge number of young girls who eventually grow into women—women who will most likely struggle to respect themselves.

For me, because of the psychological and emotional abuse I suffered as a teen, I struggled with self-doubt for years. It wasn't until well into my adult life that I finally had an *aha* moment.

What I realized was that changing my relationship with self-doubt was my responsibility. It had nothing to do with the other people in my life.

I needed to love ME.

Taking away the power from my What-if Whisperer had everything to do with me and the relationship I had with the woman I saw in the mirror. This singular aha moment became the foundation upon which I began building my confidence.

That moment taught me that building confidence starts with something deeper: self-respect. Not surface-level praise or achievements, but the way you see yourself when no one else is watching. And it turns out, that kind of self-respect isn't just important. It's essential.

As a child, I was taught to respect my teachers, my elders, and my peers. But I can't remember ever being taught that the most important person I needed to respect was myself. When we don't respect ourselves, it becomes nearly impossible to build lasting confidence. Psychological research has shown that self-respect, closely linked to self-esteem and self-efficacy, is directly tied to how we see ourselves and what we believe we're capable of.

Albert Bandura's research on self-efficacy found that people with a stronger belief in their own abilities are more resilient in the face of setbacks, more willing to take healthy risks, and more likely to pursue meaningful goals.[8] Similarly, a longitudinal study published in the *Journal of Personality and Social Psychology* found that higher self-esteem predicted greater life satisfaction and coping strength over time.[9]

In other words, self-respect isn't just a feeling—it shapes how we act, what we tolerate, and whether we believe we're worthy of something better. And yet, emotional and psychological abuse erodes that foundation from the inside out. You start to internalize the voices around you until they sound like your own.

But just because a voice is loud doesn't mean it's right. Especially when it's tearing you down. Respecting yourself starts by noticing how you talk to yourself. How you forgive yourself. How you show up for yourself, especially after pain.

That's REAL confidence. Not performance, not perfection, but self-respect rooted in truth.

CHANGING YOUR FOCUS CAN CHANGE YOUR LIFE

We've all looked at ourselves in the mirror and felt disappointment at times with the reflection looking back at us. It's rare to find a woman who hasn't. It's challenging to respect yourself when you know all your flaws, weaknesses, and pain points. After all, you are the only one who lives inside your head.

As women, there are always a thousand and one things we can find about ourselves that we don't like. Looking in the mirror just makes those flaws more obvious since they are literally staring us in the face. For some, it is a very painful experience.

But what if it doesn't have to be?

What if you were able to look into the mirror and respect the woman staring back at you every single time? I'm here to tell you that it's possible. But first, you have to fix the root of the problem.

I believe there are several reasons why we struggle to respect ourselves. Many of those reasons have to do with societal pressures. Others have to do with relationships and the complexities that go along with them. Still others have to do with limiting beliefs. However, I think one of the biggest reasons we struggle to respect ourselves is because of *comparison*, which leads to a lack of self-worth.

When you look in the mirror, how often do you start comparing yourself to the photoshopped images in magazines and perfectly posed selfies on social media?

It makes it difficult to be proud of who you are and what you see in the mirror when you are constantly comparing what you believe to be your worst parts to the picture-perfect parts of others. It's hard to respect who you are when you're only seeing the shining moments and not the struggles and flaws that other people have.

However, if you could change your focus, you would for the better. The hard truth is that we ALL have flaws, and we ALL struggle. Even more, we all experience relationships that make it difficult for us to respect ourselves.

But you can't let those chapters of your life dictate your whole story and destroy your confidence. Similarly, you can't let self-limiting beliefs and comparisons keep you from becoming the person you were meant to be.

If you have told yourself for far too long that you are not capable and that you are not worthy, stop listening to those damaging thoughts. Not only are they hurtful, but they are eroding your confidence in a big way.

I'm here to tell you that *you are enough! You are capable! You are worthy!* And, perhaps most importantly, *you deserve respect*—especially from yourself.

These positive and powerful thoughts are what you need to focus on. Focus on all you *are* instead of all those things you think you're not. As you truly start to believe these words, your focus will shift in a positive way, and slowly, you will build your confidence.

CONFIDENCE COMES FROM WITHIN

Confucius said, "Respect yourself, and others will respect you."[10]

For so many women, respecting others comes naturally. Respecting ourselves feels like the real challenge. And too often, that challenge is fueled by self-doubt.

Going back to my relationship with John—his cruel words and actions caused me to doubt everything about myself. My confidence was completely destroyed because every day I heard disparaging words and cutting remarks.

He made me feel I was unattractive. He made me feel I wasn't smart. He made me feel that I needed him and couldn't do anything on my own. Above all, he made me feel unworthy because I was giving so much, and he still didn't like me. All that I could give—everything that I had—wasn't enough to keep him happy.

Sadly, I blamed myself for all these things. I felt that they were all my fault and that he was right about almost everything.

Honestly, I think that's what a lot of women do. We blame ourselves for whatever others think we lack, even if it's not true. This is a terrible cycle to be in and challenging to come out of. This kind of thinking really damages your self-worth and chips away at your confidence.

Self-doubt can affect so many things in both your personal and professional life. It can cause you to lose a promotion at work, to feel that you are the problem in your relationship, and ultimately, stop you from showing up as yourself and making the impact only you can make on the world.

But there's a beautiful shift that happens in your life when you start respecting yourself: others start respecting you too.

Respect starts with YOU—honoring boundaries, owning your worth, and standing behind your ideas. It's not about *demanding* respect for others but *demonstrating* it to yourself. And that shift changes everything.

Respecting yourself isn't about developing a "me complex" or thinking that you're better than everyone else. Rather, it's about understanding that you are worthy enough to deserve respect. It's also about asking yourself what you want and believing that you are worthy of it. It's having that belief in yourself that builds your confidence—little by little—until you are once again standing on solid ground.

Confidence is an inside job, and it begins by respecting your own reflection. Once you start respecting yourself, you will find that others begin to treat you differently too.

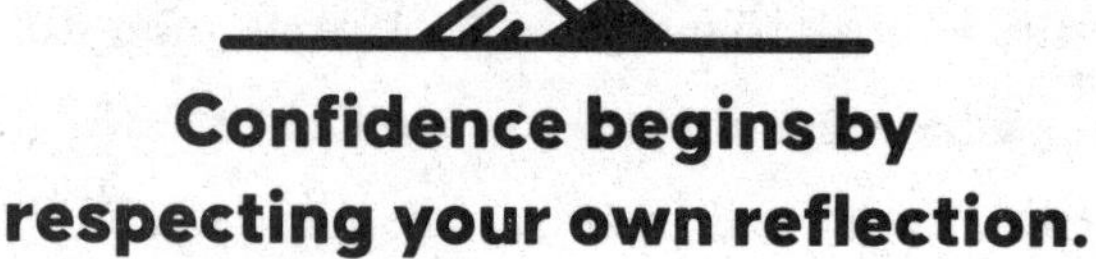

Confidence begins by respecting your own reflection.

Of course, not everyone is going to respect you—just like not everyone is going to like you. But when you respect yourself, you make it clear how you expect to be treated.

If you struggle with confidence, let me be bold for a moment: You deserve to have more faith in yourself. You deserve to trust that the woman staring back at you is capable, worthy, and stronger than she knows. Every day, you need to look in the mirror and say, "I am worthy of ___________," and fill in the blank with whatever it is you want.

For women struggling in a relationship, this may look like standing in front of the mirror and saying, "I am worthy of love. I am worthy of kindness. I am worthy of respect from my partner."

For me, at eighteen, it meant having difficult conversations and trying to express what I was feeling, even when it felt impossible. And in the end, I walked away from John and that relationship—not because it was easy, but because he was verbally and physically abusive. I had to leave in order to respect myself, even though it took me a long time to believe I was worthy of that respect.

I didn't know it at the time, but that first step toward self-respect would take me somewhere I never expected to find. It turned out that self-respect is the stepping stone to self-fulfillment and REAL confidence.

For some women, this may look like standing in front of the mirror and saying, "I am worthy of that promotion. I am worthy of the job I desire. I am capable of meeting every requirement that it asks for."

It may involve leaving a job that you are way overqualified for. Or applying for a job you might feel *underqualified* for, because you know you can do it even if you don't have all of the technical qualifications they're looking for.

Respecting yourself means understanding your value and making sure that you accept nothing less than all that you deserve.

In essence, REAL confidence doesn't come from having all the answers about who you are. It's not about *certainty*. It comes from being willing to keep showing up—curious, honest, and open to embracing all the parts of you as they unfold.

RECOGNIZE YOUR VALUE

It may not be true for everyone, but many men are raised to believe in their value from an early age, while many women are taught to question theirs. A KPMG study of more than 3,000 women in the

United States found something eye-opening: Most of us were not raised to see ourselves as leaders. Eighty-six percent said they were taught to be nice growing up. Only 44 percent were encouraged to be a leader. And just 34 percent were told, or even encouraged, to share their point of view.[11] That kind of conditioning can run deep. For many of us, unlearning it becomes part of the work of building REAL confidence.

An internal document from Hewlett Packard stated that when applying for a position at their company, men are confident in their abilities and will apply to the job if they have met just 60 percent of the requirements. Women, on the other hand, won't apply unless they have met 100 percent of the qualifications asked for.[12]

That's staggering—to think that men feel confident in their ability at just 60 percent, but women feel they have to be 100 percent "perfect" to apply. This means that if you are undervaluing yourself and your abilities as a woman, you are missing out on incredible opportunities for career advancement.

If you're a woman who works in the home, I know you face many of the same struggles. You have these incredible talents of teaching children, organizing a home, and managing finances—all transferable skills that would be celebrated in any workplace. And yet the thought creeps in: *Who am I to have a career? I'm just a stay-at-home mom.*

I told myself this for a long time. My husband is a doctor, and he's a really good one. For years, I said things like, "I'm just Rob's wife," or "I'm just a stay-at-home mom." It wasn't that those roles weren't meaningful; they absolutely were. But I had started to define myself *only* through them.

Somewhere along the way, I stopped seeing myself as Simone Knego.

I didn't realize how much of my identity I had pushed aside.

As a woman, you need to recognize that you are capable, you are valuable, and you are worthy. You need to figure out what it is you want and believe in yourself enough to go after it. It's about taking that first step.

Even if you don't meet every requirement for a job, you are absolutely capable of doing that job. It leaves room for growth. If you were 100 percent qualified for the job, you would actually be overqualified because there is no room for growth in a position you know inside and out.

You learn, grow, and gain confidence by stepping outside of your comfort zone. You don't have to know everything to begin. You learn through the process.

This is the same principle for any woman who believes she's not good enough, smart enough, or qualified enough.

The truth is, *you are*.

As a woman, you need to value what you bring to the table in every aspect of your life. You should be full partners in your relationships, valued coworkers in your jobs, and respected pillars of your community.

By understanding your value and knowing what you want, you are showing greater respect for yourself and for the things you can contribute. With that new understanding of who you are and what you can contribute comes a greater measure of confidence.

HOW TO RESPECT THE WOMAN IN THE MIRROR

We've all struggled at one time or another with the woman in the mirror staring back at us.

But what if you truly valued that woman?

What if, instead of picking apart her flaws, you focused on everything that's good and strong and beautiful about her?

What might change then?

What if you treated her with kindness and love and showed her the respect she actually deserves?

How would it change your life if you transformed the way you saw the woman in the mirror?

How would it strengthen your confidence?

Fortunately, it starts with something simple: respecting yourself.

Not in a loud or flashy way, but in the quiet choices you make every day to show yourself that you matter.

The word *respect* has a couple of meanings: "A feeling of deep admiration for someone, or something elicited by their abilities, qualities, or achievements,"[13] or the verb, "To admire someone deeply as a result of their abilities, qualities, or achievements."[14] I really love these definitions because they are a great framework to help you learn how to better love and respect yourself.

You need a deep admiration for yourself. You can do this by focusing on your abilities, qualities, and achievements, and by not focusing on the things you haven't tried, acquired, or achieved.

There are going to be things you admire about others that you will probably never be or have. For example, I can hope all I want to be taller, but that is never going to happen (unless I'm wearing heels or standing on a platform). I have to be okay with that, and that's a huge part of what respect actually is—being okay with the things you *aren't* while embracing all the wonderful things you *are*.

This means you may never be a soccer mom, a CEO, or the life of the party. But maybe you're that thoughtful mom, an excellent office worker, or the people-watcher who can find the one person in a crowd who feels out of place and help them feel seen, heard, and loved.

Stop dwelling on what you aren't, and start noticing all the good you're already doing—because it's there, even if you don't always see it. Ask yourself:

- *What are some of my strengths—even the quiet ones?*
- *What makes me me—the things no one else does quite the same way?*
- *What are the moments, big or small, that I'm truly proud of?*

Here, I'll start—because I want you to feel how real this is for me too. What's one of my strengths? I'm pretty good speaking to large crowds. I still get nervous, but I genuinely enjoy it. Maybe it's because I love people. I love hearing their stories, talking with them, connecting, and sharing my own stories too.

What am I proud of? One of my greatest achievements is my family. My husband and my children are my favorite people in the world. They've shaped my life in ways I'll always be grateful for. They remind me, every day, of what really matters.

When I focus on those things—my strengths, my qualities, my accomplishments—I feel different. When I stand in front of the mirror and *really* acknowledge them, I feel lighter. Happier.

More confident.

More in love with the woman staring back at me.

And this can happen for you too.

I invite you to take a moment and make a list of your abilities, your qualities, your achievements. Start recognizing them when you look at the woman in the mirror. And here's the thing—if your best friend read this list, she would be amazed. If you were reading this list about her, you would be just as amazed. So why not believe that you deserve to be amazed by yourself too?

When you make this a regular practice, your confidence will grow. Not because you've changed who you are, but because you finally chose to *see* her.

KEEPING IT REAL

RESPECT STARTS HERE

PROMPT

What's one choice you've made that helped you reclaim your self-respect?

____

____

____

EXERCISE

Think of a time when you stood up for yourself—whether it was walking away, setting a boundary, or speaking your truth.

Now, complete this sentence in your journal:

"When I chose myself, I realized I was ____________

______________________________________."

Then, write three things that moment taught you about your strength.

1. ______________________________________
2. ______________________________________
3. ______________________________________

Chapter Three

HONOR AND BE TRUE TO YOU

"Always be a first-rate version of yourself instead of a second-rate version of somebody else."[15]

JUDY GARLAND

I once read something that said, "Labels are for wine bottles."

I'm not sure who said it, but I'm pretty sure they were right. Labels *are* for wine bottles—not for people.

Labels are for wine bottles–not for people.

And yet, we label ourselves and others from the moment we wake up to the moment we go to sleep. Without even realizing it, those labels start to stick. And once they do, they're hard to peel off. Worse, they start to shape how we see ourselves. They chip away at our confidence—quietly, consistently.

As I said in the last chapter, when we look at ourselves in the mirror each morning, instead of focusing on the good, we often find those things we don't love about ourselves. Sadly, those things stick out like a sore thumb, and we stay focused on them because they bother us. They are the things about ourselves that we struggle with the most, and we just can't seem to let go of them.

Some of these things aren't even physical flaws. As a matter of fact, most of the things we struggle with probably aren't even flaws at all. They just look or act or feel differently than we think they ought to.

Whether it's our weight, our body, our intelligence, our bank account, or any other attribute or characteristic we don't like, we fixate on those things. And with such a negative focus on everything we don't like, we give ourselves unfair and unkind labels.

Labels are the things you call yourself in your head, where no one else can hear. They are the tags you attach to yourself when you are describing the person you think you are. They are the negative things other people have said to you that have deeply affected the way you see yourself.

There are also labels that society puts upon us based on what we look like, where we live, how we speak, what our education is, or how much money we make. These labels, whether good or bad, have a huge impact on who we are and how we see ourselves.

These labels can create self-limiting beliefs, lead to self-doubt, and slowly strip away your confidence until you have no confidence left. The labels you give yourself become the limits you live within.

The labels you give yourself become the limits you live within.

If you want to grow your confidence, it's vital that you let go of negative labels and stop letting them define how you see yourself.

HOW DO YOU SEE YOURSELF?

When you think about who you are—*really* are—what comes to mind?

Do you picture a woman who's driven, caring, and resilient? Do you see someone who juggles a thousand responsibilities and still shows up for the people she loves? Do you recognize your own strength, your progress, your quiet wins?

Or …

Do you zero in on your flaws? Do you label yourself as lazy, dramatic, too much, or not enough? Do you focus on the ways you think you're falling short, instead of everything you're carrying, everything you've already overcome?

How you *see* yourself shapes how you *treat* yourself. It shapes what you believe you deserve. And it shapes what you're willing to ask for, go after, and fight for. You can't change your life if you keep calling yourself names that don't belong to you.

You can't change your life if you keep calling yourself names that don't belong to you.

If you want to shift your self-image, start by getting curious:

- *What story are you telling yourself about who you are?*
- *What labels are you still holding on to that no longer serve you?*
- *Who has impacted the narrative of who you are, and is their input trustworthy?*

Every word you use to describe yourself matters. These words become labels that subconsciously determine how you present yourself to others and how you show up in the world.

Because we are human, we spend a lot of our time putting ourselves in boxes, trying to define who we are. Similarly, we go around trying to put other people in boxes and stamping labels on them without even realizing what we are doing.

But remember, labels—and boxes—are for wine, not for people. (Can you tell that I like wine?)

All the terrible things you say to yourself or about yourself will negatively impact every other aspect of your life if you continue down that harmful path. What you say to yourself every day influences your self-concept and dictates the direction of your thoughts and actions. These negative thoughts are dangerous. You are essentially sabotaging your own confidence. By disrespecting who you are, you become your own stumbling block.

This is why it's not only important for you to recognize the labels you are putting on yourself but to also understand how those labels are influencing you.

LABELING THEORY PSYCHOLOGY

In psychology, *Labeling Theory* is the theory of how our behavior and identity are influenced by the labels (or words) we use to describe ourselves. There are two parts to Labeling Theory: *positive labeling* and *negative labeling*.

The concept of positive and negative labels may seem obvious or simplistic, but they have monumental power over us. Whatever labels we use to describe ourselves, positive or negative, will stay with us and determine the outcome of our lives.

Negative labeling is basically talking bad about yourself, both in your own head and out loud to others. It's not only who you think you are, it's also who you tell other people you are. By using negative labels, you are undermining yourself in every way, shape, and form. It is self-sabotage at its very core. For example, if you keep telling yourself that you are useless, you are most likely going to be less effective in your efforts. The same results will come from any kind of negative label you give yourself.

Labels such as Poor, Weak, Ugly, Selfish, Lazy, Fat, Unworthy, Loser, and Stupid are all negative labels that could lead you right into becoming exactly who and what you've labeled yourself as. In this, your negative thoughts may become your own self-fulfilling prophecy.

But the truth is, these are just arbitrary labels, and our lives are made up of so much more than that. But the negative labels we use to describe ourselves will stick with us and eventually pull us down and restrict our potential. Research shows that when people engage in negative self-talk, such as repeating to themselves, *"I can't do this"* or *"I'm not enough,"* those words do not just reflect how they feel. They reinforce it. A 2021 study found that negative self-talk was tied to measurable changes in emotional state and brain connectivity, both of which are linked to higher risk for depression and anxiety.[16] You should never give a label the power to define you as a person. Just like you should never put yourself in a box.

LABELS AND SELF-ESTEEM

For years, I looked in the mirror and threw out one negative label after another. I called myself fat and unattractive. I hated the way clothes fit me. I felt I was unsuccessful because I was "just" a stay-at-home mom.

To be perfectly honest, that label—stay-at-home mom—used to be a real challenge for me. However, it was never a *negative* label for me until others began using it in that way.

I got married at twenty-one and had my first child at twenty-four. I was still in my twenties when I went to a women's dinner, a casual event a friend had organized. I don't remember the theme or even what we ate. But I remember the room—round tables, dim lighting, the kind of event where everyone's trying a little too hard to make conversation. I remember exactly where I sat: next to a woman in a sharp blazer with polished nails and an air of authority.

We made polite small talk, the kind you do when you're seated beside someone you don't know. She told me she was the CEO of a major corporation. I nodded, impressed. Then she asked, "So, what do you do?" I smiled and said, "I'm just a stay-at-home mom." In today's acronyms, a SAHM. But in that moment, what I was really doing was justifying my life, shrinking it down into one word: *just*. She paused, then looked right at me and said, "I can't think of anything worse." Just like that. No hesitation. No softening.

I sat there, stunned—my smile still frozen in place, unsure of what to say. I managed something like, "Well, I love it. I really do. I love being with my kids." But the words felt small, like I was trying to defend my entire life in a single sentence.

The rest of the dinner blurred. I laughed at the right times, nodded when I was supposed to, but inside, I kept hearing her voice on a loop.

I can't think of anything worse.

I already carried doubts. I was already asking myself if I was "doing enough." And in that moment, she confirmed the fear I hadn't dared to say out loud: that maybe what I was doing didn't count. That maybe *I* didn't count.

Being a mom, in general, comes with a whole slew of defining labels—single mom, helicopter mom, tiger mom, curling mom, free-range mom, outsourcing mom, attachment mom, working mom, and on and on. And typically, these labels given to moms are not positive. There are negative implications that go along with all these labels given to mothers.

If you're a working mom, you don't spend enough time with your children. If you're a stay-at-home mom, you sit around and eat bonbons all day long. If you're a helicopter mom, you worry too much about your children.

No matter what kind of mom you are, it seems that you just can't get it right.

And what about the women who make the choice not to have children at all? Or if you are unable to have biological children, that comes with a label as well. Either you're selfish for not wanting to have children, or something is wrong with you if you can't.

It seems that no matter what we do as women, there's a label involved with it.

Sadly, if we listen to these labels and then use them to label ourselves on a regular basis, these labels can become very damaging to us and affect our confidence and self-esteem at a core level.

WOMEN AND IMPOSTER SYNDROME

You've probably heard the term *imposter syndrome* thrown around, but maybe you've never thought much about it or wondered if or how it has popped up in your life. Put simply, imposter syndrome is the constant inability to believe that your success is something you deserve or legitimately achieved because of your own skills and efforts.

This is something most of us have experienced at some time in our lives. As a matter of fact, studies have shown that an estimated 70 percent of women have experienced imposter syndrome at work.[17]

That is a heartbreaking statistic. So many women don't give themselves credit for what they've accomplished. No matter how much they do, or how well they do it, they downplay their success, chalking it up to luck, timing, or someone else opening the door. The truth is, it's often self-doubt quietly working behind the scenes, making them feel like outsiders in their own lives, like they haven't *earned* the space they've already claimed.

The harsh reality is, imposter syndrome is something made up of our own insecurities. And we're not alone. Even the people we look up to the most have struggled with imposter syndrome.

Michelle Obama is one of those people. During a UK book tour, she spoke at a North London school and shared her honest feelings about not feeling good enough. Discussing her time as a student at Princeton, she said:

> I had to overcome the question "Am I good enough?" I overcame that question the same way I do everything—with hard work. I decided to put my head down and let my work speak for itself. I felt like I had something to prove because of the color of my skin and the shape of my body, but I had to get out of my own way . . . . [Imposter syndrome] never goes away. It's sort of like, "You're actually listening to me?" It doesn't go away, that feeling

> of "I don't know if the world should take me seriously; I'm just Michelle Robinson, that little girl on the south side who went to public school."[18]

So, yeah ... EVEN Michelle Obama struggles with imposter syndrome. We all struggle. We all question whether we are enough.

Instead of assigning labels, to ourselves or to other women, we can choose something different. We can focus on *elevating* one another. On lifting ourselves and each other up. Because when we do that, we're not just building our own confidence; we're helping others build theirs too. More lifting. Less labeling.

More lifting. Less labeling.

The world needs more of that.
More lifting. Less labeling.

THE POWER OF SELF-ACTUALIZATION

I mentioned earlier that Labeling Theory psychology includes two types of labels: positive and negative. You might have noticed, though, that I only really discussed the negative. Or maybe you didn't notice. Maybe it felt perfectly natural to only think of negative labels we apply to ourselves. Maybe you couldn't even imagine harnessing that psychological power to achieve something good for yourself. Isn't it interesting how easily we run toward the negative and too often miss the positive?

Using positive labeling—words that include praise and encouragement—changes your behavior and the beliefs you have about yourself. When you use labels like *hardworking*, *motivated*, and *successful*, you can't help but start to see yourself in a more positive light.

When you assign yourself positive labels and do all you can to live up to those labels, you will start to act and think according to the positive labels you've given yourself.

Some examples of positive labels are Smart, Friendly, Generous, Kind, Compassionate, Capable, Beautiful, and Successful. There are many positive things that you can say to yourself to strengthen your resolve and build your confidence.

The labels you use to describe yourself should be words of praise and encouragement. They should be labels that make you feel good about yourself, boost your confidence, and empower you to do more.

From my perspective, these really aren't labels at all. Instead, they are positive words of affirmation that you can use to encourage yourself to be the very best you can be.

It's about self-actualization.

People who like themselves tend to be kinder to both themselves and others.[19] Studies in psychology and neuroscience have shown that self-compassion is strongly linked to greater empathy, emotional resilience, and more positive relationships.[20] Why? Because when you see yourself through a compassionate lens, it changes how you show up in the world. It softens your inner dialogue, which makes it easier to offer patience and grace to others too.

Liking yourself also improves your mood and overall satisfaction with life. Research consistently shows that self-acceptance and self-respect are key contributors to long-term well-being and happiness.[21] There's a quiet confidence that comes from feeling at peace with who you are—and from that place, joy feels a lot more possible.

When you start seeing yourself through a more positive lens, something shifts.

You begin to cut through the noise—the negativity, the doubt, the comparison—and finally see who you really are. There's real power in that kind of perspective. It deepens your self-worth, giving you the confidence to show up as you, fully and unapologetically.

CHOOSE TO SEE YOUR WORTH

If simply changing the labels we place on ourselves can make such a profound impact on our lives, how do we peel off the old, negative labels we've grown so comfortable with and replace them with new, positive labels that speak light and life into our sense of self?

It starts in the same place we keep coming back to: the mirror.

Stop picking yourself apart whenever you look at yourself. You don't need anyone—especially yourself—pointing out every flaw, imperfection, or insecurity. *I'm ugly. My smile is weird. My nose is too big. My hips are too wide. My chest is too small. When did I start getting whiskers? No one could ever find me attractive.*

You would never speak to a friend that way. Heck, most of us would never even say those things to someone we absolutely despised. So … why would you say these terrible things to yourself? Do you deserve less of your kindness than the person you like least in the world?

All of these negative labels chip away at your confidence bit by bit until there's practically nothing left. Few of us would actively choose to hurt ourselves in this way. If someone asked you if you'd rather feel good about yourself or feel bad about yourself, I doubt you'd say, "Oh, bad. Definitely bad. I really want to feel as worthless as I possibly can." But that's exactly the decision we're making every time we stick one of those negative labels on ourselves. We are guaranteeing that we'll feel a little worse about ourselves today than we did yesterday.

Don't do that. Even if you've looked at yourself that way your whole life, don't do it anymore. It's not the only option. It doesn't have to be your default position, your go-to self-talk. You can change the way you feel about yourself, and it starts by changing the way you see yourself.

When you choose to view yourself through a lens of kindness, something powerful happens:

- You start to see the good.
- You start to recognize the strength that was always there.
- You start to believe those positive labels.

By shifting your mindset and changing the story you tell yourself, you can unlock a new way of living—one rooted in respect, not criticism. And no, I'm not talking about just lying to yourself. And respecting yourself isn't about liking everything you see on the surface. It's about honoring the whole woman you are: the work you pour into your days, the relationships you treasure, the dreams you're still chasing, the beliefs, talents, and hopes you carry in your heart.

It's about where you've been and where you're determined to go.

Above all, it's about respecting your strength, your worth, and your journey. You have every reason to be proud of who you are. Whether you're a single woman, a stay-at-home mom, a working mom, a single mom, a working woman without children, an empty nester, a widow, or retired—whatever season you're in—your worth doesn't need to be defended or explained.

You don't have to fit into someone else's box.

You don't have to *earn* your self-worth; you already deserve it.

And just as importantly, we as women need to stop labeling each other. We are not wine bottles meant to be categorized and shelved. We are wildly different, beautifully unique, and worthy of celebration.

The most powerful thing you can do is quiet the voice inside that tries to tear you down. You don't have to listen to the What-if Whisperer. You don't have to believe her. You don't have to obey her. You get to choose a different narrative—one that honors who you truly are.

I want you to really think about this. If we can believe the negative things we say to ourselves every day, why can't we believe the positive things? Who would you be if you gave as much weight to your strengths as you do to the things you believe are your flaws?

That critical voice may never disappear completely, but it doesn't have to define you anymore. It doesn't get to steal your confidence. It doesn't get to tell your story.

Whether we're CEOs, celebrities, or stay-at-home moms—every one of us wrestles with doubt and self-criticism. But you can choose kindness instead. You can choose honesty over perfection. You can choose to be real with yourself and the world around you.

When you respect yourself, embrace your failures, ask yourself what you want, and live without limits, you don't just survive; you thrive.

MIRROR MOMENTS

One of the ways I have learned to be real with myself is by practicing what I like to call Mirror Moments, when I pause and look intensely and with purpose at the woman in the mirror—not to pick myself apart, but to really *see* myself. When I stop zeroing in on what I don't love and start noticing what I do, I remember who I am and why I'm worth showing up for. Mirror Moments are opportunities for you to focus on those things you know are your superpowers while also recognizing how you are making a difference in the world. They are times for you to stop fixating on everything you think you *aren't*, or everything you *can't* do, and start focusing on what lifts you up. This is your time to focus on the wonderful things that make you uniquely *you*.

In my Mirror Moments, I make a point to find three things I like about myself. Sometimes it's something small, like the way my eyes crinkle when I smile. Other times it's something deeper, like how resilient I've become.

I encourage you do the same (even if it feels awkward and forced). The next time you're in front of a mirror, take a moment. Look at the woman staring back at you, and find three things you love about her. She's worth noticing, and she deserves your respect.

Now, as I've shared this practice with other women and invited them to try it, I've had some say to me, "What if there's not one thing I like about myself?"

Okay, ladies ... I just don't believe that's possible. We all have something worth seeing. Just because you can't see it right away doesn't mean it's not there. It might just mean you've spent too long focusing on what you *don't* like, and you've forgotten how to see what's already good and valuable in you.

It could be your eyelashes.

Your smile.

Your sense of humor.

The fact that you got up this morning and *showed up*—tired, overwhelmed, and still going.

It might even be that you're wearing your favorite shirt and you like how it feels.

Whatever you can find that reflects something real and true about *you*, start there. Because when you learn to focus on your strengths, your presence, and your resilience—anything that reminds you that you matter—it creates momentum. And that momentum can carry you through even the hardest days.

When you find something you like, don't just think it; say it out loud. Speak it into the world. Proclaim it. Write it in your journal, or start a new note in your phone's Notes app called "Things I Like About Myself." Record whatever you come up with during your Mirror Moments, and get in the habit of going back through the list regularly. You need to remind yourself what you're capable of. Remind yourself of your strengths and stop giving so much power to your weaknesses.

Remember, we all have negative labels we've stuck on ourselves. Every single one of us. What separates the people who move forward from the ones who feel stuck isn't the absence of struggle; it's where they choose to place their focus.

What separates the people who move forward from the ones who feel stuck isn't the absence of struggle; it's where they choose to place their focus.

LET GO OF THE LABELS

If you want to move forward in a positive direction and experience REAL confidence, you have to let go of the labels. You have to stop trying to fit into someone else's version of who you're supposed to be, and start being true to *you*.

Because that kind of confidence?

It doesn't come from outside approval.

It comes from owning who you are—fully, imperfectly, and honestly.

If we want to get real with ourselves, we must look beyond the surface, and beyond the things we struggle with, to recognize the strength, value, and potential that already lives within us.

We need to be proud of who we are and who we are becoming. This is what Mirror Moments are all about. The more you practice respecting your reflection, the easier it becomes to respect yourself. And the more you respect yourself, the more naturally you'll show up as the real you.

Day by day. Step by step.

Your confidence will grow—until it becomes unshakeable.

KEEPING IT REAL

REWRITE THE LABEL

PROMPT:

What's one label you've put on yourself that no longer fits who you are?

____

____

____

EXERCISE:

Write down one negative label you've carried.

____

Ask yourself:

- Where did this label come from?
- How is it hurting you?
- Who would you be without it?

Now cross it out, big and bold—and replace it with a truth:

"I am not ____________. I am ____________."

Display the new label somewhere you'll see it this week.

Chapter Four

THE WAY YOU SPEAK TO YOURSELF MATTERS

"Talk to yourself like you would to someone you love."[22]

BRENÉ BROWN

Words are powerful.

Words are powerful.

How you use them matters.

There are so many ways we tear ourselves down, often without even realizing it. You'd be hard-pressed to find a woman who hasn't, at some point, used her own words to chip away at her confidence.

Here's a stat that always stops me: According to The Dove Self-Esteem Project, only **2 percent** of women worldwide consider themselves beautiful.[23]

Two percent.

Meanwhile, **65 percent** of Americans believe in aliens.[24]

So, let's just sit with that for a moment: the typical woman is *twenty-one times* more likely to believe in little green men than to believe that she's beautiful.

Aliens? Absolutely.

The beauty of her own reflection? Not so much.

It's ridiculous. But it's also exactly why this conversation matters.

The problem starts early. More than half of American girls, 53 percent, are unhappy with their bodies by the age of thirteen.[25] By seventeen, that number jumps to 78 percent.[26] And nearly 30 percent of women are still dissatisfied with their bodies at sixty.[27]

It doesn't end there.

About 80 percent of women say they struggle with low self-esteem, and many believe it holds them back in their careers.[28]

According to the 2021 Women's Confidence Report, most American women say they need *external validation* in order to feel confident.[29]

Why is that? Why do we believe we need someone else's words to feel good about who we are? When you put all of that together, it's absurd. From the time we're barely teenagers all the way into our sixties, we're still carrying this same story of not being enough. Why do we accept that? Why do we keep believing it? From the time we're barely teenagers all the way into our sixties, we're still carrying this same story of not being enough.

From the time we're barely teenagers all the way into our sixties, we're still carrying this same story of not being enough.

What if we flipped that? What if you became the positive, encouraging voice inside your own head? What if you were the one reminding yourself of your worth? I'm not talking about toxic positivity or pretending everything is fine when it isn't. I'm talking about speaking to yourself with the same honesty, compassion, and encouragement you'd give someone you love. That's not fluff. That's self-respect. Speak to yourself with the same honesty, compassion, and encouragement you'd give someone you love.

Speak to yourself with the same honesty, compassion, and encouragement you'd give someone you love.

How would that shift your beliefs? How would that change the way you walk into a room, show up in a relationship, or go after something you want?

Because when you let the words of others determine your worth, you're handing over your power. And chances are, you're giving it to someone who may not use it with care.

No one knows you like *you* do. You know your story. You know your strengths. You know the voice in your head. You are the expert on you. So why not keep your power in the hands of an expert?

Yes, it's nice to get a compliment every now and then. But if you want REAL confidence, it must come from you. Speak kindly to yourself. Be your own encourager. Talk to yourself like you would your best friend.

Confidence built from within is the kind no one can take away.

Confidence built from within is the kind no one can take away.

YOUR WORDS MATTER

Researchers at Queen's University in Canada developed a new way to track thought patterns and estimated that we have about 6,200 thoughts every single day.[30] And psychologist Fred Luskin suggests that as many as 80 percent of those thoughts are negative and 95 percent are repetitive.[31] Which means most of what runs through your mind on any given day is the same self-critical message playing on repeat.

If you constantly tell yourself, *I'm not good enough,* or *I always mess things up,* or *I'll never be confident like her*—your brain starts playing that message on repeat. Not once. Not twice. But hundreds, maybe even thousands, of times a day.

Eventually, your mind doesn't question it anymore.

It accepts it as truth.

Before you realize it, that "truth" shapes the way you see everything—your body, your worth, your relationships, your choices.

And that's not just harmful to you. It affects the way you show up for everyone you love. When you don't believe in yourself, it becomes harder to receive love, to set boundaries, and to pursue the things that matter. So, if your thoughts are on repeat, let's start changing the track.

A while back, I was standing in front of the mirror, getting ready for an event—and completely picking myself apart.

I had gained some weight, and nothing in my closet felt good. The clothes I had tried on were either too tight, unflattering, or just plain uncomfortable. I tugged at the hem of my shirt, twisted from side to side, hoping to find a flattering angle.

And then the words started.

"I can't believe I let myself gain weight again," I muttered.

"Everyone else at this event is going to look amazing, and I'm going to look … like this."

"Why do I always do this to myself? Why can't I just keep the weight off?"

It spiraled quickly, just like it always did. The same cruel banter I had spoken to myself so many times before. The same disgust. The same disappointment.

I didn't just think those things; I *said* them out loud.

To the mirror. To my reflection.

Harsh. Unfiltered. Familiar.

And then—my fifteen-year-old daughter walked in.

She stopped in the doorway, looked right at me, and said, "First of all, Mom, you're beautiful. Second of all, you need to stop."

She didn't say it with judgment.

She said it with love. And urgency.

Then she said something that hit me like a punch to the chest:

"You're giving me a complex. How am I supposed to love my body if you don't even like your own?"

I froze, tears filling my eyes.

She didn't raise her voice. She didn't need to. Her words cut through the noise in my head because I knew she was right. What we say to ourselves doesn't stay with us. It spills into the room. It lands on our children and teaches them how to see themselves.

If my daughter kept hearing me talk to myself like that, what kind of voice would she develop in *her* head?

That moment changed me. Not all at once. Not overnight. But it woke me up. I started being more intentional with my words, even when I was alone (or thought I was).

I practiced looking in the mirror and finding something kind to say, even if it felt awkward at first. I knew that if I wanted my daughters to see their beauty, I had to be willing to see mine.

No filters, no Photoshop, no excuses, and no apologies.

The REAL *me*.

Getting there is easier said than done, though. Learning to quiet your negative self-talk isn't easy. We have a natural tendency to focus on what's wrong, what's missing, what's flawed, what's not enough. Negativity has a way of sneaking into our thoughts and making itself at home.

If we wrote down every negative thing we said to ourselves in a day, it would be overwhelming, maybe even heartbreaking. But if you want to respect yourself and grow your confidence, you have to learn how to interrupt that cycle. Those thoughts keep you stuck, chip away at your belief in yourself, and create a mental environment where confidence can't thrive.

Letting go of that inner criticism won't happen overnight, but when you begin to loosen its grip, something powerful happens: you make space to notice what's steady, strong, and true about you. And when you focus on those parts of yourself—your real traits, your resilience, your worth—you give confidence room to grow.

My own experience with negative self-talk is exactly why I created a tool to help myself and others start to shift those thought patterns, because the way you talk to yourself matters. And learning to speak to yourself the way you'd speak to someone you love—well, that might just change everything.

THE POWER OF CTRL-ALT-DELETE

Your ability to overcome negative thought patterns might be simpler than you think. It starts with three keys:

Ctrl. Alt. Delete.

If you've ever used a Windows computer, you might remember this classic combo. When things froze or stopped working, you'd hit

Ctrl-Alt-Delete to reset the system. It didn't erase everything; it just gave you a clean slate.

(If you're a Mac user, think of this as the "Okay ... now what?" moment when everything crashes and you just hit the power button and reboot.)

I started thinking, *What if we could do the same thing with our mindset?*

What if you had your own reset button when the What-if Whisperer takes over, when your confidence glitches, or when the same old thoughts keep dragging you down?

It turns out—you do. And it's the same familiar key combo:

Ctrl. Alt. Delete.

Three simple keys. One powerful shift.

Three simple keys. One powerful shift.

Let me explain.

CTRL: Control the Narrative

The first step is awareness. You have to notice the negative thoughts as they show up, because you can't change what you don't recognize.

Once you *see* them, you can stop them.

You can interrupt the pattern and take control of the words you're using. You can't change what you don't recognize.

You can't change what you don't recognize.

I'm so stupid.

Pause. Replace it.

I made a mistake, but I'm still learning.

This is how you take the power back—not by pretending the thoughts don't exist, but by refusing to let them take over.

ALT: Choose an Alternative

Alt stands for alternative, and there is *always* an alternative.

There's always another way to think, to speak, to believe.

Never forget that the words you use shape your reality. So, if you speak in limits, you'll live in limits. But if you speak in possibility, you expand what's possible.

If you speak in limits, you'll live in limits. But if you speak in possibility, you expand what's possible.

So, shift the script:

- I can't do this. → I was made for this.
- What if I fail? → When I succeed, what doors will open?
- I'm not ready. → I've come too far not to try.

- I don't belong here. → I earned my seat—and I'm not giving it up.
- I always mess things up. → I've learned more from my failures than most people do from their wins.

This isn't about toxic positivity; it's about choosing thoughts that fuel your growth, not your fear.

Speak to yourself like someone who believes in your potential, because there's always an alternative—and you get to choose it.

DELETE: Clear the Mental Clutter

Now, it's time to delete the beliefs that don't serve you.

The ones that tell you you're not smart enough, strong enough, worthy enough.

The ones that keep you shrinking, doubting, comparing.

Imagine hitting delete on every thought that holds you back.

Every lie you've told yourself.

Every outdated version of who you're "supposed" to be.

Delete the comparison game.

Delete the belief that you are not enough.

Delete the idea that you need to change who you are.

Then, install something new.

Replace that clutter with thoughts that reflect your truth.

Thoughts that say:

I am capable.

I am growing.

I am more than enough.

Ctrl. Alt. Delete.

Three simple keys.

One powerful shift.

This is how you break the loop, reset your mindset, and start building REAL confidence—the kind that doesn't need permission, perfection, or approval.

POSITIVE AFFIRMATIONS ARE KEY

If you had asked me about positive affirmations ten years ago, I would've rolled my eyes and told you they were all woo-woo nonsense, that there was no science behind them and they definitely didn't work.

Today, I know better.

I've learned that positive affirmations are not only powerful; they really are backed by science.

I use them daily, and this one simple practice has transformed how I see myself. It turns out, our brains are far more adaptable than we think. Thanks to something called *neuroplasticity*, the brain can actually rewire itself in response to new thoughts, experiences, and beliefs. This means the words you speak *to* yourself and *about* yourself matter.

MRI scans show that when people practice self-affirmation, the parts of the brain tied to reward and self-worth actually light up. These include the areas that process motivation and meaning.[32]

The science is real.

The impact is real.

And I've felt it firsthand.

Further research has discovered that through the repetition of positive and affirming statements, the brain can form new neural pathways—a process of rewiring itself.[33] This means that every time you repeat positive statements, you are essentially creating a *physical* connection to those positive thoughts. You are literally *changing your brain*.

What does that mean for you? Well, when you use positive affirmations daily, you are strengthening your neural pathways, making it easier for your mind to return to those positive thinking patterns instead of falling back into negative thinking. In other words, you are creating a positive path for your thoughts to travel.

Rather than subconsciously pumping your head with negative words and phrases that run on repeat all day, you can consciously and intentionally fill your mind with positive words and phrases to train your brain to believe those things instead.

As you make positive affirmations a regular daily practice, your brain will naturally go to those positive affirmations because you have made them the neural path of least resistance. Once this becomes a habit, your brain will more naturally stay focused on the positive.

Over time, this practice can lead to increased self-esteem and greater confidence.

Research has shown that positive mental and physical outcomes are often a natural result of our ability to regulate our thoughts.[34]

Some studies have even found that when we regularly use positive affirmations, we're more likely to view challenging situations as meaningful and worth engaging in, rather than something to avoid.[35]

With so much science supporting their power, it's no surprise that more and more people are starting to incorporate affirmations into their daily lives.

TRAIN LIKE AN ATHLETE

We all know that athletes train their bodies intensely to stay at the top of their game. But what many people don't realize is that the best athletes also train their minds. Positive affirmations have become a powerful tool in the world of sports—not because they're trendy or magical thinking, but because they work.

Sports psychologists have found that what athletes say to themselves, especially under pressure, can significantly impact their performance.[36] While it's not a replacement for physical training, mental training is a critical part of the full picture. When athletes combine physical preparation with tools like affirmations, visualization, and mental focus, they're more likely to perform at their highest level and recover faster from setbacks.

Take Sunisa Lee, Olympic gold medalist and one of the most celebrated gymnasts in the world. Before competitions, she repeats a grounding affirmation to help her focus: "Nothing more, nothing less. Your normal is good enough."[37]

It's not about being perfect. It's about trusting who she already is. That phrase helps her stay centered and reminds her to perform like she's practiced—not to push for more, but to let her excellence speak for itself. Affirmations like these are part of the mental toolkit she uses, along with journaling and visualization, to build confidence, stay calm, and show up strong.

Simone Biles, arguably the greatest gymnast of all time, has also been open about using affirmations, especially on days when the pressure feels overwhelming. Her go-to mantra is, "You've got this. It's your time."[38] These are more than just words. They're grounding reminders that help her steady her mindset, even in the most intense situations.

Valarie Allman, a two-time Olympic gold medalist in the discus throw, uses this mantra: "I am capable of winning. I deserve to win. I will win."[39]

When she first started saying it, she admitted it felt awkward, like maybe she didn't fully believe it yet. But she kept saying it. Out loud. Over and over. Eventually, something shifted. She found herself repeating the words throughout the day without thinking. She began to carry herself differently. And before long, she actually started seeing herself as a winner—not just hoping she could win, but expecting to. That's the power of repetition. That's the power of language.

It's not just athletes either.

Jennifer Lopez has shared that her day doesn't feel complete without at least fifteen minutes of affirmations. One of her go-to mantras is: "I am beautiful and timeless at every age. I am enough."[40]

She credits affirmations as a key part of her success and her sense of grounding. In fact, she surrounds herself with positive words. No, I haven't been to J.Lo's house, though I wouldn't turn down an invite. But I've read enough interviews to know affirmations are woven into her décor, from the cushions to the wall hangings to the trays. They're part of her environment, a constant reminder of who she is and the mindset she's committed to.

What I love about all these examples is that none of these women are *pretending* to be confident. They're *training* for it.

They're practicing it.

They're speaking it into existence.

Even if it feels awkward at first …

Even if the words don't land right away …

They keep saying them. And so should you.

Your brain is listening.

And eventually, it starts to believe you.

Jennifer Lopez isn't the only celebrity who uses positive words to shape her perspective of herself. Alicia Keys' mantra is, "I love myself as I am."[41] Maya Angelou's famous mantra was, "Nothing can dim the light that shines from within."[42]

Some of the world's most powerful and influential women use affirmations daily, and they often credit the practice with shaping their success. They know that the words they speak to themselves and about themselves are what shape their reality. They also know that believing in who they are is the greatest gift they will ever give themselves, and that confidence begins with the words they think and speak.

PRACTICE MAKES PERFECT

Once you recognize the importance of positive affirmations, it's important to remember that, just like anything that is worthwhile, it will take time.

One positive affirmation isn't going to take all the negative thoughts away. A week of daily affirmations isn't going to be enough to counteract a lifetime of negative thought cycles. It will require practice on your part.

You don't go to the gym once and become a bodybuilder. You don't take one Spanish lesson and become fluent. You don't play one note on the piano and become a concert pianist. All these things take practice and repetition for you to see positive results that stick.

It's exactly the same with positive affirmations. The success of self-affirmations rests largely on repetition. As a matter of fact, according to a recent study, people are more likely to consider repeated information true rather than statements they've heard only once.[43] So if you want to actually believe the positive affirmations, it's important to repeat them over and over again.

This is why taking even just a few minutes a day to repeat positive affirmations can create a powerful shift in your confidence. It's not just about saying nice things—it's about the *practice* of speaking to yourself with intention. When you consistently speak words that affirm your strength, your worth, and your potential, those words begin to take root. And the more you say them, the more you start to believe them.

As you begin using affirmations in your daily routine, one of the most important things you can do is say them while looking in the mirror. Not just to check a box, but to *see* yourself as you speak. It might feel awkward at first. You might even avoid eye contact with your reflection. But that Mirror Moment matters. It's where the shift begins. When you look yourself in the eyes and speak life over the woman staring back at you, something powerful happens. You move from *saying* the words to actually *feeling* them.

In the beginning, you'll say these affirmations because you want them to be true. You'll be reaching for belief. But with time and repetition you'll begin to notice a change. You'll start to recognize those truths in yourself, and your confidence will grow. Not because someone else told you you're enough, but because *you* did.

Eventually, you'll look in the mirror and recognize the woman standing there—someone who's not only *trying* her best, but who is *becoming* her best. Becoming more confident. More grounded. More whole. You'll see the extraordinary, unordinary woman you were always meant to be.

This may be the very first time you actually see yourself—I mean *really* see yourself. Not the flaws or the comparisons, but the strength. The growth. The grace. You'll begin to see someone worth loving, and you'll start to believe it.

That might just be the beginning of everything.

THE FIVE I'S

If you're not sure where to start with positive affirmations, I totally get it. It can feel awkward or forced, especially in the beginning.

So, before I share the affirmations I use personally, I want to give you a little background that really helped shift my mindset.

There's a well-known piece of research from relationship expert Dr. John Gottman that talks about something called the five-to-one ratio. His studies showed that in a healthy relationship, for every one negative interaction between partners, there needs to be at least five positive interactions to balance it out. That's the ratio for connection, trust, and long-term health: five to one.[44]

Gottman's work is mostly applied to marriages and work environments, but when I first heard it, my immediate thought was: *What about our relationship with ourselves?*

How we talk to ourselves matters just as much (maybe more) than how anyone else talks to us. If you're constantly feeding yourself negative thoughts—whether it's criticism, self-doubt, comparison, or shame—you're going to need a whole lot of positive reinforcement to shift that internal balance.

That's where affirmations come in. They're not just motivational phrases or fluffy mantras. They are *your words*, intentionally chosen, spoken with purpose, and repeated with care. They are your chance to rewrite the narrative you've been living with and to start seeing yourself in a new light.

When I began using affirmations, it wasn't because I fully believed the words I was saying. It was because I wanted to. I needed to. And the more I practiced, the more I noticed a shift—both in how I felt and how I treated myself. The words I spoke started to feel like the truth. My truth.

That's what I want for you too.

When we look in the mirror, the very first thing we often see as women is something negative.

The flaw. The wrinkle. The thing we wish we could change.

It's heartbreaking, really, how quickly our minds go there.

For many of us, it's become so automatic that we don't even realize we're doing it.

We scan for what's "wrong" instead of recognizing what's *right.*

Like I mentioned earlier, it's often the things we don't like about ourselves that stare back at us the loudest. But it doesn't have to stay that way.

So, here's my challenge to you: When you look in the mirror, don't give your mind time to go to that negative place.

Interrupt it.

Redirect it.

Take that moment and fill it with words that speak life into who you are—words that train your brain to see the good.

For me, this started with something I call my Five I's. These are five powerful affirmations I say out loud in the mirror to shift my mindset and start my day with intention.

Here they are:

- I am strong.
- I am beautiful.
- I am smart.
- I am worthy.
- I am more than enough.

These Five I's have carried me through tough days, helped me reset my thinking, and reminded me of who I truly am. When I speak them with intention, really looking myself in the eyes as I do, it changes the tone of my entire day. It's not about faking it until you make it. It's about saying it until you become it.

It's not about faking it until you make it.
It's about saying it until you become it.

Now, these are *my* words. They may not be *your* words, and that's okay. Your Five I's should be as unique as you are. They should reflect the strength you carry, the woman you are becoming, and the truth you want your mind to believe. So, take some time to write your own Five I's, five "I am" statements that ground you, lift you, and help you see the woman in the mirror with more kindness and clarity.

As you think through this exercise, remember:

- These affirmations don't have to reflect what you feel in the moment.
- They can reflect what you hope to feel.
- They can be aspirational.
- If you're feeling anxious, say, "I am calm."
- If you feel uncertain, say, "I am grounded."
- If you're struggling, say, "I am healing."
- This is about speaking to your potential, not your perfection.

To take this a step further, try visualizing yourself living out each affirmation. For example, when I say, "I am strong," I picture myself lifting weights or doing something that pushes me physically or mentally. When I say, "I am happy," I see myself laughing with my kids. (Yes, chaos and joy can live in the same house!)

Whatever affirmation you choose, pair it with a mental image.

See yourself in that truth.

Feel it.

Own it.

This practice—saying my Five I's out loud while looking myself in the eye and picturing the reality of my words—has changed my life. I believe it can change yours too.

When you start training your brain to see what's good, to speak what's possible, and to claim what's true … little by little, day by day, you'll begin to build something that no one can take from you. It's not about faking it until you make it. It's about saying it until you become it.

That's what I call REAL confidence.

WE NEED TO STOP JUST-IFYING OUR LIVES

Before I close this chapter, there's something I feel like I have to say. It's not a tip or a tool; it's something I lived, and it has everything to do with how I used to talk about myself.

For years, I used the word *just* to describe who I was.

"I'm *just* Rob's wife."

"I'm *just* a stay-at-home mom."

"I'm *just* a board member."

"I'm *just* an ordinary girl."

I used it like punctuation. Like padding.

It softened the impact, because I wasn't sure if saying those things out loud without apology would sound important enough. I wasn't sure *I* was important enough.

Looking back, I realize that little word carried a lot of weight.

Just became the way I explained myself without actually standing in who I was. It was how I tried to preempt other people's judgment: before they had the chance to think I wasn't doing enough, I'd go ahead and say it for them.

The truth is, I wasn't trying to *describe* my life. I was trying to *justify* it. And I didn't even know I was doing it.

I think a lot of women do this, especially when we don't feel like we measure up to some invisible standard we never agreed to in the first place. We use words to downplay ourselves. We soften, we shrink, we explain. But here's what I've learned: You don't need to defend your life. You don't need to apologize for the role you're in. You don't need to slap a *just* in front of it to make it acceptable.

If you're a bookkeeper, you're a bookkeeper.

If you're a stay-at-home mom, you're a stay-at-home mom.

If you're working part-time, full-time, building a business, or keeping a household together, you're doing something real, something worthy, something enough.

The more I started paying attention to the way I described myself, the more I realized how much it was feeding my self-doubt. Once I removed that one little word—*just*—everything shifted.

I started hearing myself differently.

I started seeing myself differently.

Little by little, I stopped apologizing for being who I was.

So, here's my encouragement to you:

Take the *just* out of your story.

Take it out of your sentences.

Take it out of your self-worth.

Say who you are—and let that be the end of the sentence.

Not a justification. Not a defense. Just the truth.

Because you matter. And you don't need to shrink to be accepted.

Drop the JUST.

KEEPING IT REAL

FIVE KIND THINGS

PROMPT:

What would change if your inner voice became your biggest encourager?

EXERCISE:

Start a Mirror Moment practice this week.

Each morning, look yourself in the eyes and say *five kind things* out loud. If you get stuck, try:

- I am proud of ...
- I am grateful for ...
- I am becoming ...

Write down how you feel after seven days. What shifted?

PILLAR #1 EXERCISES

RESPECT YOU-RSELF

If you truly want to learn how to respect yourself, it's time to put your learning into practice. Here are ten different exercises to help build your confidence by respecting yourself. Choose one of these exercises and follow through with it. You can come back and choose a different exercise as often as you need to. Remember, self-respect begins where self-sabotage ends, so don't skip these exercises. They are an important part of building REAL confidence.

1. SELF-TALK AUDIT

Spend a day tracking your inner dialogue. Write down self-sabotaging thoughts as they arise. At the end of the day, reframe each negative thought into a statement of self-respect or encouragement. For example, replace "I can't do this" with "I'm capable of learning and improving."

____

____

____

2. ACTION OVER PERFECTION

Identify one way you tend to self-sabotage—maybe it's procrastination, perfectionism, or overthinking. Set one

small, realistic goal for today and take action on it without second-guessing yourself. When you do, pause and celebrate the progress.

___

___

___

3. SELF-SABOTAGE TRIGGERS LIST

Write down common scenarios or emotions that lead you to self-sabotage (e.g., fear of failure, comparison, or overwhelm). For each trigger, create a self-respect response. For example:

- Trigger: "I feel unworthy when I compare myself to others."
- Response: "I focus on my own unique progress and accomplishments."

Trigger:

___

Response:

___

Trigger:

___

Response:

___

4. DAILY "VICTORY" JOURNAL

At the end of each day, write down one thing you did well, no matter how small. This exercise helps shift focus from perceived failures to acknowledging wins, reinforcing self-respect.

____
____
____

5. PAUSE AND PIVOT TECHNIQUE

When self-sabotaging thoughts arise, take a deep breath and ask, *Is this thought helping me?* If not, pivot by stating a thought or action that aligns with self-respect.

6. RESPECTFUL BOUNDARIES PRACTICE

Identify one area where you consistently overextend yourself (e.g., saying yes to every request). Practice saying no in a respectful way that prioritizes your well-being.

7. REWRITE YOUR NARRATIVE

Take a situation where you felt you self-sabotaged in the past and write a new version of the story as if you had acted with self-respect. Reflect on how this shift in behavior could have led to a different outcome.

____
____
____

8. VISUALIZATION EXERCISE

Close your eyes and imagine a moment when you typically self-sabotage. Visualize yourself responding with self-respect instead. Feel how empowering it is to choose self-respect over self-sabotage.

9. THE "SELF-RESPECT ALARM"

Set an alarm on your phone with a message that encourages self-respect (e.g., "You deserve to succeed" or "Choose respect over sabotage"). Use this reminder to realign your thoughts and actions throughout the day.

10. SEEING THROUGH SOMEONE ELSE'S EYES

Find someone you trust and ask them what they love and respect about you. Write down their answers and reflect on them whenever you are struggling to respect yourself. Visualize seeing yourself through their eyes.

____

____

____

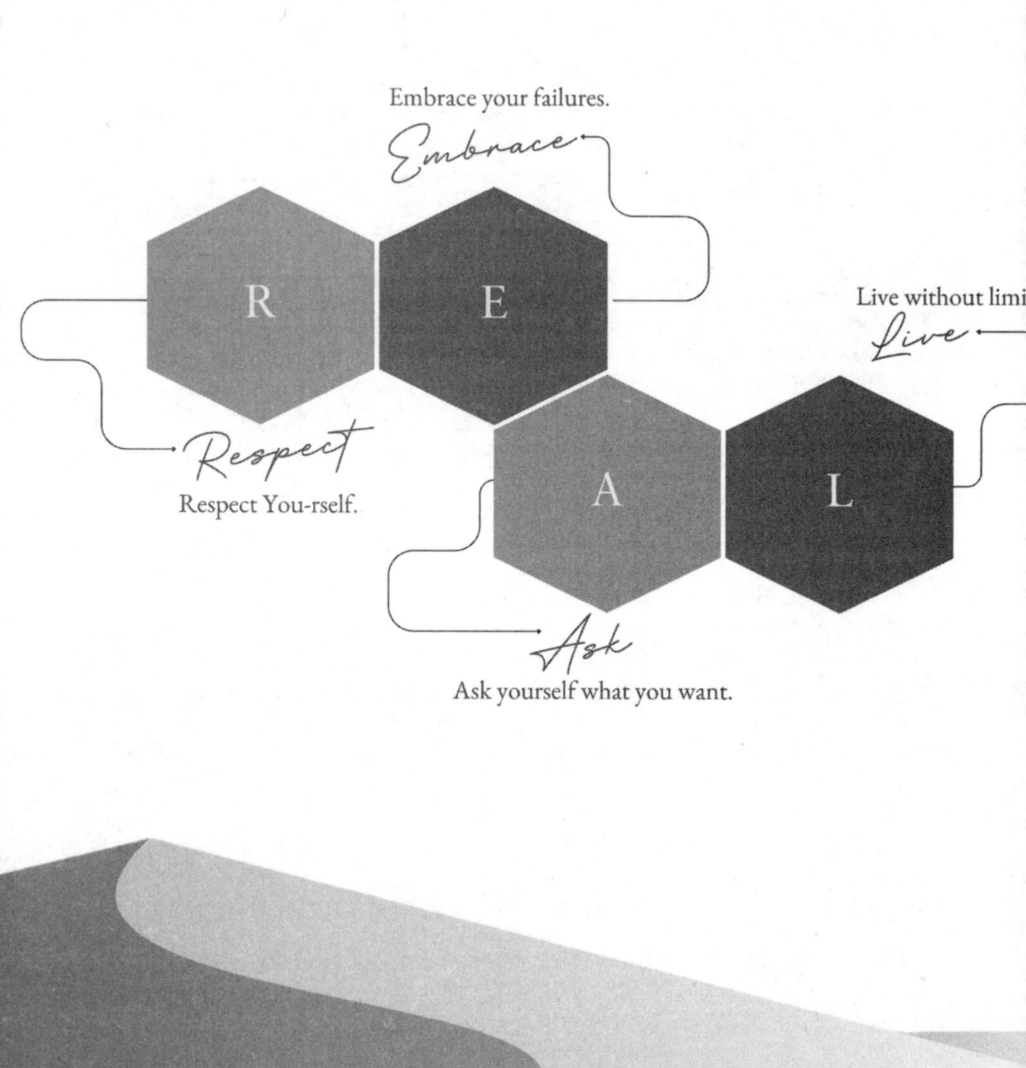
Embrace your failures.
Embrace
R
E
Live without limi
Live
Respect
Respect You-rself.
A
L
Ask
Ask yourself what you want.

PILLAR #2

EMBRACE YOUR FAILURES

Embracing failures is an essential part of personal growth. It allows us to learn, adapt, and become stronger. The courage to grow comes from your willingness to try, even when success isn't guaranteed. Each stumble or setback is an opportunity to discover what didn't work, refine your approach, and build resilience. By viewing failures as stepping stones rather than roadblocks, you create the freedom to take risks and explore your full potential. Growth isn't about perfection—it's about progress, and that begins with the bravery to step forward despite the fear of falling.

Chapter Five

ALLOW YOURSELF TO FAIL

"It's not how hard you fall, but how high you bounce that counts."[45]

ZIG ZIGLAR

When it comes to failure, I'm a big believer that you get stuck or you get strong. Failure, for me, has been about learning from my mistakes and moving forward. I can't say it was always that way for me, but I've learned over the course of my life that this is the mindset you need to have if you want to build REAL confidence.

You get stuck or you get strong.

DON'T LET FAILURE CONTROL YOU

Your confidence takes a hit every time you allow failure to control you. Then, after you've taken enough hits and your confidence is low, you stop moving forward. That's when you get stuck—second-guessing, overthinking, and hesitating.

Over the years, as I've matured—and certainly after I survived my fair share of failures—I had an epiphany: By the time you realize you've failed at something, it's already in the past. It happened. It's over. No matter how much you replay it in your mind, you cannot change the outcome.

But there *is* something you *can* change: what you do next.

Sometimes, without even realizing it, we carry our failures like baggage. Instead of learning the lesson and letting it go, we hold on. We carry that failure around with us. We beat ourselves up. We let that failure define us. The longer we hold on, the heavier it becomes. It starts to dictate our future actions, self-worth, and willingness to try again.

Some people say you "fail forward." But really—it's not the failure that moves you forward. It's what you do after.

You have to stop gripping so tightly to your failures that they kidnap your confidence and hold it hostage. Yes, failure is hard. Yes, it can knock the wind out of you. You're allowed to feel that. You may need a minute to process, catch your breath, and recover. That's okay—but don't stay down too long. The longer you stay there, the harder it is to rise. At that point, you lose focus and motivation, and confidence becomes harder and harder to find.

That's why every time you fall, you have to get back up—even if it's slow and even if it's messy. That is how you build confidence: not by avoiding failure, but by refusing to let it define you.

The best way to overcome failure?

Change the way you see it.

WHAT DID YOU FAIL AT TODAY?

Sara Blakely, the founder of Spanx, grew up with a father who understood the importance of failure and the growth it can bring us. Every day at the dinner table, her father would ask one simple question: "What did you fail at today?"[46]

If Sara couldn't think of anything she had failed at, like tripping in the locker room or missing some questions on a math test, her father would be disappointed. That one question, "What did you fail at today?" helped Sara reframe failure as proof that she was trying new things and seizing opportunities. If she wasn't failing, her father reminded her, she wasn't really trying.

With this mindset, experiencing failures became a positive thing and nothing to be ashamed of. Sometimes, her best failures were even rewarded with a high-five from her proud father. For Sara, the greatest tragedy wasn't failure; it was never trying or risking anything.[47]

Oftentimes, it's your own thoughts and fear of failure that hold you back from accomplishing the things you really want to achieve in life. That is, the *fear* of failing can be much more paralyzing than having to deal with *actually* failing!

The best way to overcome your fear of failure and gain greater confidence is to regularly ask yourself the same question Sara's father asked her: "What did you fail at today?"

This question is a great way to reframe failure as something positive and even helpful. The more you fail, the more you grow. And the more you see failure as something positive, the more confidence you will have to keep on trying. Remember, failing at something doesn't make you a failure. It means you tried.

Failing at something doesn't make you a failure. It means you tried.

IF YOU FAIL, TRY, TRY AGAIN

When Sara was in college, she dreamed of going to law school. She took the LSAT and did horribly. Determined to improve, she studied harder and tried again, but her second score was even lower.

Although she felt defeated, she decided to pivot and chase another longtime dream: performing as a character at Disney World. Sadly, she was two inches too short to fulfill her dream of being Goofy, so she was cast as one of the Chip and Dale Chipmunks instead.

After her acting stint ended at The Most Magical Place on Earth, she went back to her hometown and took a job selling fax machines. Her ultimate dream, though, was to create a product that would help people feel good. That dream became Spanx.

Sara stumbled many times along the way, but she never gave up. She may have failed at things, but she was never a failure. And that's the difference: Failure is something you experience, not something you are. Today she's built a billion-dollar brand that's helped millions of people feel more confident in their own skin.[48]

Failure is something you experience, not something you are.

It's important to understand that getting back up and trying again doesn't mean you have to stick with the same exact goal. You don't have to keep banging your head against something that isn't meant for you—unless you're absolutely sure it's what you want.

Sometimes, a goal simply isn't attainable—no matter how hard you try. No matter how much Sara wanted it, there was no way she was going to grow two inches to fit into that Goofy suit. But that didn't mean she failed; it just meant she had to pivot.

Letting go of what's not meant for you doesn't make you a quitter. It makes room for what *is* meant for you. Trying new things is what brings variety, growth, and excitement into your life. And often, that's exactly where confidence is built—in the trying.

IT'S OKAY TO CHANGE YOUR MIND

I was premed while in college at the University of Florida. It wasn't my *dream* as much as it was everyone's *assumption*. My parents were both physicians. My sister became one too. So, naturally, I was expected to follow the same path.

I was strong in math and science throughout high school, so it didn't seem like a stretch—until I took organic chemistry. From the start, it just didn't make sense to me. I studied. I stayed after class. I did everything I could to get a handle on it, but I failed the class. That was tough, but I wasn't ready to give up, so I retook it.

The reward for my dedication and stick-to-itiveness? I got a D.

And as anyone on the premed track knows, there's no med school without organic chemistry.

That failure shifted everything. It was one of those moments where life grabs you by the shoulders and says, "You're not going this way anymore." This was more than a simple closed door. This experience pushed me to ask a very big question: *If not this, then what?*

I've had many friends ask me if I regret not being able to go to medical school, and I'll admit I spent many years feeling the sting of that failure. But I haven't regretted it in a very long time, because I always seem to find something that interests me just a little bit more.

I've done a lot of different things in my life, and I'm a big believer that it's okay to change your mind. That's part of being human. You are *allowed* to change your mind. There are so many different directions you can go, and you don't have to "get it right" on the first try.

You don't have to keep doing the same thing, but you *do* have to keep doing *something*. That's how you build confidence and keep moving forward. Each time you fall, pick yourself up, brush yourself off, and take the next step. That's progress.

After I failed organic chemistry, I switched to accounting. I had dreams of being an actress, but my dad told me that as long as he and my mom were paying for college, I needed to choose something more "reasonable." (How ridiculous is that?)

I was always good at math, so accounting felt like a logical next step. I ended up getting both my bachelor's and master's in accounting, and I passed the CPA exam on my first try. Back then, there were four parts, and you needed a 75 on each one to pass.

My scores: 75, 75, 75 … and 79. I definitely overstudied for that last section.

I started my career and worked as an accountant for a while, but I eventually had to be honest with myself: I didn't love it. At all. I spent my days crunching numbers, staring at spreadsheets, and wondering if this was what I was meant to do. I kept thinking, *There has to be more than this.* And listen, shout-out to the accountants who light up when they see a spreadsheet—you're the reason the rest of us survive tax season. And while numbers weren't my passion, I held on to the dream of doing something that truly made me feel alive.

After we had our first child, everything shifted. We moved out to the country—wide open skies, quiet mornings, and space to breathe. I've always loved horses, and ever since I was a little girl, I pictured myself one day owning a horse farm. So I decided to go for it.

I started small—teaching riding lessons to kids after school, boarding a few horses for friends, and eventually building out a full summer camp. There was something magical about watching the kids grow in confidence with every ride. I loved every part of it—the early mornings in the barn, the smell of hay, the joy on a child's face after their first trot.

That little horse farm gave me a new sense of purpose. For a season, it was exactly where I was meant to be. But seasons change and so do dreams. Before long, we packed up and found ourselves in Florida, stepping into a brand-new chapter.

WHEN DREAMS FAIL, DREAM ANOTHER DREAM

We moved to Florida just eight weeks after I gave birth to our second child. I wasn't working outside the home then, as I was knee-deep in diapers and Cheerios, doing the work that no one sees but everyone depends on. Then came our third baby, and life got even fuller.

But somewhere between nap schedules and laundry piles, I felt that tug—that whisper that said, *There's more for you than this.*

So, when a friend asked if I wanted to start flipping houses, I jumped at the chance. It felt exciting. Purposeful. Like a new way to contribute to our family.

We bought fixer-uppers. We paid contractors. We split costs. And we made some truly terrible decisions.

One of the worst came during a season when I was already stretched too thin. The housing market was hot. Homes were selling fast, and we jumped on a property without doing the kind of research we normally would. I had just had knee surgery, and I wasn't paying close attention to the details.

At first glance, the house seemed like a solid investment. It was older, but we thought we could fix it up and flip it like we had done before. But not long after we started, problems came to the surface. The electrical system was a mess. And then we discovered a large tree in the yard that we weren't legally allowed to remove because it was protected. That tree blocked everything we had planned.

We had already poured money into the house by the time we found out. We couldn't renovate it the way we intended, and there was no way to recover what we had invested.

That house became the tipping point. The numbers stopped working. We couldn't keep up with the payments. The bank took the houses back, and we were left with the mess.

That mess wrecked our credit—not just mine, but my husband's too. Even though I was the one running the project, he also got hit with the consequences. That broke me.

I felt sick with guilt, like I had dragged him into my failure, like I had risked too much and ruined something we'd worked so hard to build.

We were reminded of that failure every time we tried to finance anything. I remember sitting in a dealership, getting denied for a car loan, and feeling my stomach drop.

The voice in my head wasn't gentle.

You did this. You ruined this. You should've known better.

And yet … my husband never once made me feel that way.

He wasn't angry. He didn't yell. He didn't blame me or hold it over my head.

That was all me.

I carried the guilt like it was mine alone to bear, like it somehow proved I wasn't enough. It showed the world that I'd failed at the business, as a wife, as a mom, and as a woman trying to do something meaningful.

No one talks about the shame that sticks around long after the dust settles. The shame of letting yourself down, even when no one else says a word.

But here's the truth I had to learn: Failure is part of the process.

And guilt? Guilt is a heavy weight that only holds you back if you let it.

I had to forgive myself. Sure, what happened mattered; it had a big impact on my life. But I mattered too. I had to stop letting that failure *define* me and start using it to *refine* me.

Even when you're full of confidence, you're going to fail sometimes. But when you do, confidence helps prevent you from letting that failure be the end of the story.

After the house-flipping fiasco, I took a step back professionally. I needed time to regroup financially and, probably more importantly, emotionally. I threw myself into motherhood, fully focused on raising our growing family. As part of that journey, we made the decision to adopt. Adoption has been one of the most life-changing and beautiful parts of my story, but it's too big to tell fully here. I share much more about that journey in my first book, *The Extraordinary UnOrdinary You*.[49]

Eventually, I went back to school to become a teacher. I loved it—being in the classroom, making a difference—but financially, it just didn't make sense. With six kids at home, I was paying my babysitter more than I was earning. It became clear that something had to give.

That's when I pivoted again, this time into medical sales. It was a far cry from the classroom, but it gave me flexibility and a much-needed financial boost. Plus, it opened the door to something I never expected. Through some of the volunteer work I was doing at the time, I was invited to speak on stage.

And just like that … something clicked.

I fell in love with storytelling and the stage. And for the first time in a long time, I felt fully aligned with what I was meant to do. That moment sparked a fire that led me to begin writing, sharing, and speaking professionally.

Looking back, it's wild to think that none of this would've happened if I hadn't failed organic chemistry. That one closed door rerouted my entire life, and every twist and turn eventually brought me here.

Do I still wish I could've been an actress? Absolutely. Maybe that's why I love the stage so much. It's not exactly Broadway, but let's be honest—I can't sing, and my dancing wouldn't land me in any chorus line.

Still, give me a mic and a good story, and I come alive.

When you're doing something that fuels you, confidence becomes a natural side effect. It doesn't have to be forced or fabricated; it just grows, because you're in alignment, you're lit up, you're alive.

If you're not feeling that spark right now, maybe it's time to ask yourself some hard questions.

What are you chasing—and is it still what you really want?

What's stopping you from trying something new?

Every step of your journey matters. Even the ones that feel like detours. Especially the ones that feel like failures. And failure only becomes a dead end when you decide to stop walking.

Every step of your journey matters. Even the ones that feel like detours. Especially the ones that feel like failures.

But if you choose to keep dreaming—even when it's hard, even when you're tired—those dreams have a funny way of evolving into something even better than you imagined.

So, embrace the failure. Learn from it. And then get up and dream again. The woman who keeps dreaming is the woman who keeps growing.

The woman who keeps dreaming is the woman who keeps growing.

LEARN TO EMBRACE A GROWTH MINDSET

There isn't a single person on this planet who hasn't failed. Everybody fails.

But sadly, not everyone is able to move forward from failure. Some people let it hold them back, while others use their failures to push them forward.

The difference between those who break under the pressure of failure and those who use it as momentum to propel them forward is mindset.

How you bounce back from failure is largely determined by your mindset and perspective. Do you see failure as something negative? Do you fear failure or feel ashamed because of it?

If this is you, I want you to pause and be honest with yourself. Are you letting past failures define you? Are you holding on to guilt so tightly that it's keeping you stuck? You're not alone if you are. But here's the truth: You don't have to keep carrying that weight. Let this be your moment—the moment you decide to stop giving your failures the final word. You are allowed to grow. You are allowed to change. And you are absolutely allowed to move forward, even if the past didn't go as planned.

If you truly want to achieve REAL confidence, you must learn to see failure as something positive. That is how you can use it to drive yourself forward.

You have the opportunity to learn important lessons from everything you do. Every failure you've gone through is a lesson learned and an experience gained. Life is made up of those lessons and experiences. Those lessons make you who you are.

If you pay attention, you will notice that you are constantly learning from your successes and your failures. You need them both. Sure, in the moment, it's hard to move forward from what may seem like one failure to the next. However, it's essential that you understand that those failures are teaching you valuable lessons.

Failure isn't the opposite of success; it's part of the journey to where you want to go. Rather than allowing your failures to control you, you can use them as stepping stones.

Each time you fail, even when it's really difficult, stop and ask yourself, *What have I learned from this failure, and what experience have I gained because of it?*

If you face every failure with this growth mindset, you'll be able to move ahead with confidence much more easily.

TEACH YOUR CHILDREN ABOUT FAILURE

As we learn to navigate failure as adults, we should also be mindful of teaching our kids. That might sound a little strange, but hear me out: If we want to raise confident, resilient children, we have to teach them how to fail. If we don't teach them, life will.

If children never experience failure when they're young, they're going to be in for a rude awakening when they realize, later in life, that failure is a normal, necessary part of growth.

We live in a world where trophies are handed out just for showing up. Recently, I was clearing out my son Jacob's room. He's twenty-nine now, and I was finally packing away some of the childhood keepsakes that had been sitting on his shelves for years.

My daughter Mili was helping me and said, "Wow, he has so many trophies!"

"He sure does," I laughed. "That was the participation trophy era … which, honestly, we're still in. You and your brothers and sisters all had shelves full of them." Jacob and the rest of my kids were rewarded for showing up, not for how well they played. Don't get me wrong; there's value in that. But it's also important to remember that real life doesn't hand out trophies just for showing up.

Eventually, the world asks more of us. If we don't teach our kids how to handle those moments—the ones where they don't win, don't get the part, or don't make the team—they're going to feel lost when it happens.

Failure is inevitable, but failure isn't the problem. It's how we respond to it that matters.

As parents, we have this incredible opportunity to teach our kids how to lose gracefully, how to regroup, and how to try again. We teach them how to achieve but also how to reset when they don't. That's what builds lasting confidence—not constant success but the ability to keep going, even when things don't go their way.

LET KIDS FAIL

You know those parents who complain about a teacher and demand their child be moved to another class, simply because the teacher's style doesn't quite match their child's preferences? Sometimes it's valid. Other times … it's not.

When it's not, what those parents are really doing is teaching their children that it's never their fault, that discomfort is something to escape rather than navigate. They're robbing their kids of a powerful opportunity to learn resilience.

The earlier we learn to fail, the easier it becomes to handle setbacks later on. Failure teaches us how to reflect, adapt, and move forward with confidence. When we shield our kids from every disappointment, we unintentionally send the message that struggle is something to avoid. That message chips away at confidence instead of building it.

When children are praised for everything they do—without effort, challenge, or feedback—they don't learn determination. But when they try, fail, and try again? That's when the lessons stick. That's when confidence is built from the inside out.

Failure teaches humility. It teaches focus. It teaches grit. And above all, it teaches this essential truth: Just because you didn't succeed today doesn't mean you won't succeed tomorrow.

Why am I sharing the importance of teaching our children how to fail in a chapter about embracing our own failures? Because we, as women, need to recognize that we are the example. Our kids watch how we handle disappointment. They hear the way we talk about ourselves when things don't go as planned. They learn from our reactions, whether we stay stuck or get back up.

And while I've been talking about our children, this message matters for every woman—whether you're a mom, an aunt, a teacher, a mentor, or someone a young girl looks up to. Kids are always watching. How we respond to failure—how we speak about it, move through it, and rise from it—shapes what the next generation believes is possible. Your example might be the one that helps a child learn how to try again.

If you struggle with a negative mindset around failure, I invite you to start shifting that narrative—not just for yourself, but for the next generation. Let them see that failure is a powerful teacher. That growth comes from the struggle. That trying again is not weakness, but strength.

KEEPING IT REAL

REWRITE THE STORY

PROMPT:

Think about a time you failed—a moment that still lingers in your memory. How would you talk to yourself about the bump in the road today?

EXERCISE:

Write about the same event twice.

1. First, describe it the way your inner critic tells the story.

2. Then, rewrite it through the lens of growth. What did you learn? How did it shape you?

When you shift the story you tell yourself, you reclaim your confidence. That's where real growth happens.

Chapter Six

OWN THE POWER WITHIN YOU

"You can waste your lives drawing lines. Or you can live your life crossing them."[50]

SHONDA RHIMES

Everyone has strengths. Even if you don't think you have strengths, you do. You just haven't uncovered them yet.

Sometimes, your strengths are easy for you to see. Other times, you may need others to help you recognize them.

And sometimes, you can uncover your strengths in the most unlikely of ways and in the most trying of circumstances.

REDEFINING STRENGTH

You've probably never heard of Rob Oliver.

He's not a celebrity, and he doesn't have millions of social media followers. But he has something far more powerful: a story that will challenge how you think about strength, identity, and confidence.

When I was a guest on Rob's podcast, I noticed something different about the way he spoke. He took deeper breaths. He paused more often. His words carried a kind of calm, steady weight.

And then, halfway through the conversation, he casually mentioned that he was paralyzed from the chest down.

Suddenly, everything made sense—the calm in his voice, the way he carried himself with quiet strength, the grounded confidence that radiated from every word. He had been through something life-changing, and instead of letting it define him, he let it deepen him.

When Rob Oliver was a young adult, two of his greatest strengths were his athleticism and his ability to get things done.

This strength was evident, even to strangers. For example, Rob once had two different job interviews. The first interview was at a pizza shop where they were hiring both a sandwich maker and a delivery driver. The interviewers were so impressed with Rob that he was hired to do both jobs.

Rob's second interview was with UPS. Again, the hiring team was so impressed that they hired him on the spot. He was invited to start orientation the very day.

But everything changed in a single moment.

One afternoon when he was twenty-one, Rob was body surfing on the Outer Banks of North Carolina. It was something he'd done countless times before. But this time, the wave didn't carry him in—it slammed him down.

His head hit the ocean floor. Hard.

In that instant, everything went still. His neck was broken, leaving him paralyzed from the chest down, with only limited use of his arms and hands.

His girlfriend, Becky, watched the whole thing unfold from the beach. She saw the commotion. The panic. The emergency helicopter that airlifted him to Norfolk General Hospital.

For days, he was on a ventilator. No one knew what the outcome would be.

But when he finally came off the vent, when he could speak again, the very first person he asked for was her.

And the very first thing he said?

"If you want to walk away, I understand."

Without even a moment's hesitation, Becky told Rob that what she loved about him had nothing to do with whether or not he could walk. So, he married her, and they're still together today.

After the accident, Rob's athleticism and ability to get things done looked completely different. The strengths that had once defined him were no longer available in the same way. But with the unwavering support of his wife, Rob began a new journey—one that led him to uncover even deeper strengths.

He credits Becky for helping him rebuild his foundation. She reminded him that what mattered most wasn't his physical abilities, but who he was at his core—his heart, his character, his mindset.

Rob came to understand something that many of us take a lifetime to learn: Our worth is tied to who we are, not what we can do. Stop measuring your worth by what you achieve. Start honoring who you already are. He was still Rob. He was now just living in a body that operated a little differently than the original manufacturer's design.

Stop measuring your worth by what you achieve. Start honoring who you already are.

YOUR MINDSET CAN BE YOUR GREATEST STRENGTH

Post-injury, Rob went back to college and then entered the job market with optimism. He felt articulate, intelligent, and capable of connecting with people. But after sending out dozens of applications and sitting through interview after interview, he was met with silence.

Nothing. Not a single callback.

Eventually, someone offered him a part-time role—a few hours a week. So, Rob went back to school again, this time to earn his master's degree, thinking that might open new doors. But the result was the same. Employers still couldn't see past his wheelchair. His disability walked into the room before he ever had the chance to.

And yet, he didn't give up.

He didn't let rejection define him. He didn't let silence steal his confidence. Rob held on to who he knew himself to be, and that quiet inner knowing became one of his greatest strengths.

Eventually, Rob found his way into the disability services field. From the moment the interview began, the energy was different. They saw him. They heard him. They believed in what he had to offer, and even though they only had a part-time position available, they worked to fill his schedule until he had a full forty-hour week.

He became a rockstar in that space. And he still is.

If you sat down with Rob today, one of the first things you'd notice is his mindset. He's been through something that would've broken most people—but he's one of the most positive, grounded, and quietly confident people I've ever met.

Was it hard for him to face rejection after rejection? Of course.

But he didn't let it crush him.

Instead, he learned to stop measuring his worth by other people's opinions—and that shift changed everything.

His injury may have altered his physical abilities, but it also gave him a new lens to view life. It sharpened his focus, helped him see what truly matters, and led him to his superpower: an unshakeable, hope-filled mindset.

And here's the thing: That same strength is available to you.

If you want to uncover your confidence, start by developing the muscle of a positive mindset. Like Rob, you might not see the reward right away. But over time, it will change everything—from the way you see yourself to the way you show up in the world.

YOU'VE GOT TO BELIEVE IN YOURSELF

A positive mindset begins with a belief in yourself. Rob didn't get here alone—his wife played a huge role in that. Becky reminded him of who he was when he needed it most. Her belief became the mirror he needed to see his own potential again.

That's what helped him move forward.

Life will challenge us. We'll face loss, failure, rejection, and heartbreak. But often, those same moments will teach us the most . . . if we let them.

Rob's story is a powerful reminder that we all have strengths waiting to be uncovered. In the aftermath of his accident, he drew on resilience, patience, and clarity—traits he now shares with others as an inspirational speaker.

Today, Rob uses his voice to change lives. He speaks to corporations, service organizations, churches, and schools about what it means to keep going—even when life doesn't go the way you planned. He also hosts the *Perspectives on Healthcare* podcast, where he bridges the gap between patients and providers with grace, insight, and honesty.

Rob found purpose—not in spite of his challenges, but because of them.

He's an advocate and speaker as well as a husband, a friend, and the proud father of triplets.

And through it all, he never stopped believing that he had something valuable to give.

That's what believing in yourself looks like. We often act like believing in ourselves means doing everything perfectly or pretending everything's okay when it's really falling apart. That's not it at all. Instead, believing in yourself means deciding that your story still matters. That your voice still matters. That *you* still matter. No matter what.

When you truly believe that, you'll begin the most powerful journey of all—the one that leads you back to your strengths, your confidence, and your purpose.

WHY WEAKNESS ISN'T A WEAKNESS

Sometimes, the first step to believing in yourself is simply acknowledging your weaknesses—and being okay with them. Not just okay, in fact, but *open* about them. When you're willing to share the hard parts, you give other people the courage to do the same.

I learned this the hard way.

Never in my life have I felt more inadequate than I have as a parent. There's no handbook or how-to guide that fits every child. And when you're raising more than one? Forget it. What works for one doesn't work for the next, and no two days look the same.

Parenting is, hands down, the hardest job I've ever had. And yet, from the outside, it looked like I had it all together. People would say things like, "Wow, you must be so organized," or, "I don't know how you do it."

I'd smile politely—but inside, I was freaking out.

The truth is I had very little confidence in myself. My inner voice sounded more like, *I'm such a fraud. I don't know what I'm doing. Some days, I'm barely holding it together.*

But I didn't tell anyone that. I hid it well. I wasn't trying to impress anyone, and I definitely wasn't trying to be fake; I just didn't feel like I was *allowed* to fall apart. I thought I had to be perfect. I thought struggling meant I wasn't strong.

The problem is, when you never show your struggles, no one can help you carry them. Let people in. When you share your struggles, you create connection, not weakness.

Let people in. When you share your struggles, you create connection, not weakness.

That was my biggest downfall.

It takes real strength to admit when you're struggling. It takes courage to say, "I need help." I wish I had done it sooner, because once I raised a flag, I realized I wasn't alone.

So many moms feel the same way. We put on a brave face, keep smiling, and hold it all together while quietly wondering if we're messing everything up.

But here's the thing: When you show up as your full, imperfect self, you give others permission to do the same. You create connection. You build trust. And surprisingly, you build confidence—not just in yourself, but in others too.

Real strength is about being human, flaws and all. It's about recognizing your struggles, weaknesses, fears, and failures … and showing up anyway.

GIVE YOURSELF GRACE

No matter who you are, you have strengths waiting to be discovered. But, like most of us, you probably focus more on your weaknesses, simply because they tend to shout louder. That's where the power of grace comes in.

As I've gotten older, I've learned to give myself so much more grace. However, when I was that young mom, trying to juggle everything, grace wasn't even on my radar. I was unbelievably hard on myself.

But my husband, Rob, was always very supportive. I never felt pressure from him to be a "better" mom, which is good, because the pressure I put on myself was relentless.

Looking back now, it's sobering to realize how much I struggled. I had a massive *enough* problem: I never felt like I *was* enough or could *do* enough. I didn't feel strong enough, smart enough, or emotionally tough enough.

The funny thing is, no one saw that. On the outside, I looked like I had it all together. I looked strong—because I thought that's what people expected of me. That only made things worse, though, because the pressure to keep up that illusion made it even harder to ask for help or show any cracks.

People assumed that because I had six children, I must've been some kind of superhero. They put that expectation on me, and eventually, I did too. I felt like I wasn't allowed to fall apart. I was convinced that everything in our life would crumble the second I stopped holding it all together, so I held on for dear life.

But here's what I've come to realize: We all have weaknesses. Every single one of us. Some are visible. Others are hidden. But they're there—and they don't make us any less worthy.

The day I finally gave myself permission to be imperfect was the day I started to breathe again. It was the day I stopped letting those weaknesses define me and started building REAL confidence.

Grace creates space. It allows your mind to shift from everything you think you're doing wrong to all the things you're actually doing right. It silences the inner critic just long enough for you to hear the truth: You're doing better than you think.

When you give yourself grace, you unlock the door to your strengths. You stop obsessing over your flaws, and suddenly, you can see what's already working.

Here's the best part:

Grace doesn't just make room for growth; it makes room for truth.

The truth that you are human.

The truth that you don't have to be perfect to be strong.

The truth that your weaknesses don't define you—your willingness to keep going does.

Because when you stop beating yourself up, you can finally start building yourself up. Give yourself grace—it's the only way to create space for real change.

Give yourself grace–it's the only way to create space for real change.

WE DON'T GROW ALONE

When you start getting serious about uncovering your strengths, one of the most powerful truths you'll discover is this:

You don't have to do it alone.

We all need support. We all need someone to remind us what we're capable of, especially in the moments when we've forgotten. When we're low, we sometimes think we need to dig deep and find the hidden strength buried within ourselves...but the strength we need most is often sparked by someone else's love, presence, or belief in us.

I'll never forget the first time I met our son Ari.

We had traveled across the world to Ethiopia, and as we walked into the orphanage, he was sitting at a little table eating lunch. He looked up, gave me a shy smile—and then, without hesitation, offered me some of his food. This tiny boy, who had experienced more hardship in his four years than many do in a lifetime, who was malnourished and recovering from illness, offered me what little he had.

That was Ari.

From the moment he took my hand in his, he didn't let go.

He had every reason to be guarded, to protect himself. But instead, he leaned in. He trusted. He loved. And he reminded me that strength doesn't always roar; sometimes it shows up quietly in the form of courage, generosity, and open-hearted trust.

Throughout our time in Ethiopia, I watched as Ari slowly let us into his world. I also saw how much I was learning from him.

His resilience, his spirit, his joy in the face of so much uncertainty—it woke something up in me.

We spent hours holding hands, sharing meals, adjusting to a new pace of life. There were language barriers, cultural gaps, and so many unknowns. But every moment we spent together made one thing clear:

We were growing together.

When we finally returned home, Ari discovered all the little things we take for granted—light switches, drinking fountains, the magic of clean running water. I watched his eyes widen with wonder, and I realized that sometimes, it takes seeing the world through someone else's eyes to rediscover your own gratitude, perspective, and strength.

That's the power of shared journeys.

Sometimes, the person helping you uncover your strength is three feet tall and has a mischievous smile. Sometimes, it's a stranger on a plane or a friend who shows up when you least expect it. And sometimes, it's you—showing up for someone else and, in the process, rediscovering what you're made of.

LIFE IS YOUR GREATEST TEACHER

If you had asked me when I was younger if I wanted kids, I probably would've said, "Maybe just one."

Fast forward to today, and yeah, life didn't go quite the way I planned. I didn't end up with one. I ended up with six.

But I wouldn't change it for the world.

I am who I am today because of the lessons I've learned through motherhood. Parenting has a funny way of holding up a mirror and showing you *everything*. The good, the bad, the tired, the messy. In that mirror, as I've said, I see weaknesses front and center—big, bold, and impossible to miss. But right alongside those weaknesses, I found my strengths.

Motherhood forced me to grow in ways I never expected. I've done things I never thought I could do, things I wouldn't have even attempted without these six incredible humans in my life.

And here's the truth: The strength you're looking for often hides in unexpected places, in what you thought were weaknesses, in the challenges you've faced, and in the lessons you've fought hard to learn.

When you use those experiences to support and connect with others, you're turning pain into purpose. You're turning struggle into strength.

It doesn't have to be parenting. Life teaches in a million ways.

For example, I was always good at math, but writing? Let's just say my English teacher, Mrs. Pressman, made it *very* clear that I had some work to do.

It wasn't that I lacked creativity; I actually loved telling stories. But grammar? Commas? Sentence structure?

Not my thing. And because of that, I convinced myself that writing wasn't for me. I just wasn't cut out for it.

So, I avoided it. For years.

But life has a way of circling back. And somewhere between diaper changes, carpools, and kitchen-table chaos, I realized I had a lot of stories to tell. Some are ridiculous. Some are moving. Most involve a little laughter and a lot of learning.

Storytelling became a cornerstone in my life. Not because I became perfect at grammar, but because I discovered the *power* of stories. The way they connect us. The way they heal and inspire.

Turns out, you don't need perfect punctuation to make an impact. You need to speak from the heart.

The ability to inspire through words wasn't something I ever thought I could do. That kind of gift, I thought, was for *other* people.

But I've learned you don't need someone else's permission to do something meaningful.

You need to see yourself differently. To believe you're capable. To build your confidence one small step at a time.

The more fully you show up to life, and the more willing you are to learn from it, the more your strengths will rise to the surface.

And your confidence will grow right alongside them.

BE YOU

If there's one thing I want you to take from this chapter, it's this: Be unapologetically yourself.

Your strengths and abilities are exactly what the world needs. You've been placed in your unique corner of the world to make a difference only you can make. So stop wishing, hoping, or dreaming that you were someone else. You're already enough. Be who you are. Stop waiting until you feel ready. Confidence grows every time you show up as you are.

Stop waiting until you feel ready. Confidence grows every time you show up as you are.

Let go of the unrealistic expectations you have placed on yourself and have the confidence to be the extraordinary person you already are. Above all, stop trying to change who you are because you think people will like you better. Their opinion doesn't matter. And what other people think of you is actually none of your business! There is power that comes from truly being who you are. Your authenticity will inspire other people to be who they truly are too.

I think one of my biggest accomplishments as a parent is that I've been able to teach my kids to be proud of exactly who they are and to advocate for themselves along the way.

Trust me, we've had our bumps in the road. But when I look at Noah, and when I hear him talk about being on the autism spectrum, he's not shy about it. He'll tell you he has autism. He'll tell you he has ADHD. And when he wakes up in the morning and starts messing around, he'll tell me, "My meds haven't kicked in yet." He's proud of who he is. And when he needs help at school, he asks for it—without hesitation.

It's the same for Ari and his dyslexia. He knows how to advocate for what he needs. He talks to his professors, manages his schedule, and figures out what works best so he can be the most successful human he can be.

Honestly, I could say the same for all my kids. They've learned the power of expressing themselves—and not just in quiet moments either.

Sometimes, as a parent, it's challenging when that self-expression is directed at you—especially when it's laced with sarcasm and followed by a dramatic eye roll. If you're a parent, I'm sure you've *never* had the pleasure of experiencing that! Still, it's breathtakingly beautiful when that same confidence spills out into the world. When I watch them stand tall, especially in hard moments, I feel nothing but pride.

At the end of the day, the most important priority for me as a parent is to raise good humans who can confidently embrace who they are. The only way to teach our children to do that, you may be disappointed to hear, is for us to confidently embrace who we are ourselves.

And if you're not a parent, this message still holds true: Every woman has the power to shape the world around her. Whether you're mentoring, leading, teaching, or showing up with authenticity in everyday life, you're modeling what it means to be confident, unapologetic, and real.

In the end, be yourself—and encourage the people around you to do the same.

That, alone, can change the world.

YOUR PERSPECTIVE WILL MAKE ALL THE DIFFERENCE

Let's bring it back to Rob Oliver, because his story isn't just a powerful example of strength. It's a reminder that perspective shapes everything.

Rob continues to make a difference in the world because he made the decision to focus on what he *could* do when others were focused on what he *couldn't*. Then, he found a way to do it with purpose. Focus on what you can do, not what you can't. That shift alone can change everything.

Focus on what you can do, not what you can't. That shift alone can change everything.

That mindset is what led him to set a Guinness World Record of 37 hours, 44 minutes, and 17 seconds of nonstop interviews on his podcast, *Perspectives on Healthcare*, where he spoke with 137 people from around the world to amplify diverse voices and champion more human-centered care. He took the skills he had—listening, connection, and curiosity—and turned them into something extraordinary.

He refused to be defined by obstacles.

His mindset allowed him to transform them into possibilities.

You can too.

You may not be setting a world record (or maybe you are), but you have strengths waiting to be used. You have a story that matters. And you have the ability to impact the world in ways only *you* can.

So, the next time you catch yourself wondering if you're qualified … if you're capable … if you're enough to make a real difference …

Come back to this truth:

You don't have to be perfect.

You don't have to have it all figured out.

You have to be willing to show up—with honesty, heart, and the courage to keep going.

The world doesn't need another polished version of someone else.

It needs *you*. Exactly as you are.

Because when you shift your focus from what you can't do to what you *can*, everything changes.

Your confidence grows. Your purpose deepens.

And the woman you see in the mirror becomes someone you trust, someone you believe in.

Not because she's perfect—but because she's REAL.

KEEPING IT REAL

FLIP THE STORY

PROMPT:

Think about a time when you surprised yourself with your own strength. It doesn't have to be a big, dramatic moment. Maybe it was speaking up when it would've been easier to stay quiet or simply getting out of bed when life felt heavy.

What did that moment reveal about you?

___

___

___

EXERCISE:

1. Write down three strengths you've uncovered through your life experiences—especially the hard ones. (Need help? Think about times you've had to adapt, lead, advocate, speak up, or rebuild.)

   ___

   ___

   ___

2. Now write one self-limiting belief you've carried about yourself—something you've told yourself you're not good at or not capable of.

____

____

____

3. Flip it. Reframe that belief using your list of strengths.
   - Example: "I'm not confident speaking up" becomes "I have a voice that's worth hearing—and when I speak from the heart, people listen."

____

____

____

Chapter Seven

MAKE ROOM FOR THE RIGHT PEOPLE

"Let go of the people who dull your shine, poison your spirit, and bring you drama. Cancel your subscription to their issues."[51]

STEVE MARABOLI

You might be wondering why there's a chapter about relationships in a section focused on embracing failure. Here's why: For so many of us, it's not the job, the test, or the business that makes us question our worth. It's the relationships that didn't work out. We don't just *mourn* the loss; we *internalize* it. We turn "the relationship failed" into "I failed the relationship," or worse, "I'm a failure." But here's the truth I want you to hold onto: A failed relationship doesn't mean *you* failed. It simply means it wasn't the right fit. And like any other hard thing, it holds the power to teach you something—to stretch you, grow you, and shape the next chapter of your life.

Toxic relationships can quietly and consistently chip away at your confidence. They convince you to shrink. To settle. To silence your needs and second-guess your worth. Over time, you stop recognizing yourself, not because you've failed, but because you've been conditioned to believe you're not enough. But walking away from a toxic relationship isn't a failure. It's a powerful step toward reclaiming your voice, your strength, and your sense of self. What feels like an ending might actually be the beginning of something better. Because even in the hardest moments, there is clarity and the chance to rebuild with more truth, more trust, and more self-respect.

TOXIC RELATIONSHIPS ARE ALL AROUND US

If the presence of toxicity in human relationships seems both shocking and horrifying to you, keep in mind that I'm talking about more than just romantic relationships here. This includes all types of relationships—bad friendships, abusive parent-child dynamics, destructive professional environments, and more. When you expand the circle like that, it becomes easier to see just how common these toxic relationships are. According to *Forbes*, an average of 80 percent of Americans have experienced emotional abuse in some form.[52]

And to go a little deeper, 73 percent of people stay in toxic relationships because ending them isn't easy.[53] It's hard to walk away from someone you know and love, even when you know it's not right for you to stay.

I've had plenty of toxic relationships over the years, and that includes toxic friendships. My relationship with John, which I described at the start of this book, was just one example (though arguably the most toxic one). As I've matured, I've recognized it isn't good for me to stay in these toxic relationships—but that didn't make it any easier for me to do the hard work of ending relationships I knew had to go.

Despite how difficult it is to walk away from people who were (and maybe still are) important to you, when the other person is being dishonest, controlling, or hostile, keeping yourself in a toxic environment is never the right call.

To be clear, I'm not a therapist, and I'm not telling you how to navigate your relationships. I don't know you, and I don't have any credentials that would equip me to determine what is right for you. However, I have learned through excruciating firsthand experience how devastating these relationships can be and how much destructive power they have over how we, as women, view ourselves. Pay attention to how a relationship makes you feel about yourself. That feeling is the truth, not the excuse.

Pay attention to how a relationship makes you feel about yourself. That feeling is the truth, not the excuse.

This chapter is here to help you take an honest look at your relationships, past or present, and reflect on how they may be shaping your confidence, your self-worth, and your sense of safety. You don't need to explain or justify your experiences to anyone. But you do deserve to feel respected, supported, and at peace in the relationships you keep.

THREE LIES WE TELL OURSELVES IN A TOXIC RELATIONSHIP

My toxic relationship with John taught me one of the hardest and most life-changing lessons of my life: *You cannot heal from inside the situation that's still actively hurting you.* In the same way, you cannot *find yourself* by *losing yourself* in someone else's chaos.

For example, I never could have healed from the damage John did to my sense of self-worth while I was still in the cycle of his abuse. If I wanted healing—and I did—then I had to take that first terrifying step, which was walking away from him once and for all.

If you haven't been in this position, you might think leaving is simple. In reality, it's anything but. From the outside, it could look like: *If a man ever laid his hands on me, I'd be out the door in a heartbeat.* Or: *A woman would have to be nuts to stay in a situation like that.* Sure, it seems so obvious to people on the outside. But when you're in a toxic relationship, you allow yourself to slip into denial, downplaying the pain and convincing yourself that your love will be enough to change them.

And if it's not, you hear the little voice in your head whispering, *This is my fault. He wouldn't act like this if I was worth loving well. This is just how I deserve to be treated.*

After looking back at my own experiences and hearing similar stories from countless other women, I've identified three destructive lies we tell ourselves when we're stuck in a toxic relationship:

1. We deny how deeply we are being hurt.
2. We cling to the hope that they will change.
3. We turn the blame inward, making their actions somehow our fault.

Of course, I didn't realize it at the time, but this is exactly what I did as a young woman. When John treated me cruelly, I'd tell myself, *It's not that bad. I can handle it.* When he disrespected me, I'd think, *He'll change. He just needs time.* When I thought about leaving, I'd hear myself say, *If I walk away, it will mean I failed.*

These are absolutely awful, soul-crushing, confidence-killing lies straight from the pit of despair. And the best way to counter a lie? Truth. So, here are three truths I want you to read out loud. In fact, it would be a good idea to read them aloud several times a day, every day, for the rest of your life!

THREE TRUTHS OF TOXIC RELATIONSHIPS

1. If someone is hurting you, it is a big deal.
2. You cannot change another person's heart or behavior, no matter how much you love them.

3. Walking away from a toxic relationship is not a failure. It's a victory for your future.

Strangely, that third truth can be the most challenging one for us to accept. When we're in the thick of it, we might have already lost so much confidence and self-worth that we actually feel *guilty* for leaving someone who has abused, debased, and devalued us to the point of despair. We might worry that we're hurting them or even *inconveniencing* them by leaving.

This is why I said the first step toward healing is to remove yourself from the relationship. We simply cannot see things clearly from inside the situation. It would be like trying to describe a forest while standing nose-to-bark with a tree. You just do not have the perspective you need from that close. It's only when you step back—*way back*—that you can finally see things as they really are. It's only then that you can even begin to accept the truth that:

- You are not responsible for fixing someone who doesn't want to change.
- You are not responsible for carrying the weight of someone else's wounds.
- You are only responsible for choosing yourself. For choosing your peace. For choosing your future.

Every moment you stay in a place that diminishes you, you forget the woman in the mirror who is worthy of respect, love, and joy. But every moment you choose to honor yourself—to listen to your truth—you take your power back. The moment you choose your peace over their approval, you begin to heal.

The moment you choose your peace over their approval, you begin to heal.

You always have a choice.

You can choose to stay and shrink yourself to fit inside someone else's small world, or you can choose to step into a life where you are loved, respected, and free.

You are allowed to choose yourself. And you are allowed to walk away.

WHEN THE TOXIC PATTERN IS FAMILIAR

Throughout this book, I've talked about Mirror Moments—the times we catch our own reflection and realize something needs to change.

But spotting toxic patterns isn't about a single moment. This is about the atmosphere you live in. The way you treat yourself when no one's watching. Not just your reflection—but your thoughts, your patterns, your default setting. This is about your whole self.

So, let me ask you something: If someone treated your best friend or your daughter the way you treat yourself, would you be okay with that? Would you call that love? Or would you call it what it is: a toxic relationship?

Because if you'd do anything to pull someone you love out of that kind of environment, why would you keep yourself in it?

Sometimes, we don't just end up in toxic relationships—we accept them because they feel familiar. If you've spent years criticizing yourself, minimizing your needs, or silencing your voice to keep the peace, then being with someone who does the same might not even raise a red flag. It might feel … normal. Comfortable, even.

But that's not because it's healthy. It's because it reflects how you've already been treating yourself.

That was true for me. I didn't recognize the emotional abuse in my relationship with John at first because I was already emotionally abusing myself. I ignored my boundaries. I spoke to myself harshly. I blamed myself for everything that went wrong. So when he did the same, it didn't feel shocking. It felt deserved.

That's one of the hardest truths I've had to face: Sometimes, the reason we tolerate toxicity from others is because we've internalized it first.

But just because it's familiar doesn't mean it's right. And it definitely doesn't mean you have to keep living that way. Familiar doesn't mean healthy. Choose growth, even when comfort feels easier.

Familiar doesn't mean healthy. Choose growth, even when comfort feels easier.

DO YOU HAVE A TOXIC RELATIONSHIP WITH YOURSELF?

We spend a lot of time talking about toxic relationships with other people—disrespect, control, constant criticism. But what happens when *you* are the one doing those things to yourself?

This might be the most important relationship you'll ever evaluate. If you want to build REAL confidence, the foundation has to be the relationship you have with yourself.

If you're not sure what a toxic self-relationship looks like, here are a few signs to gently consider. You might be in a toxic relationship with yourself if you:

- Constantly talk down to yourself or replay your mistakes on a loop.
- Apologize for who you are, not just what you do.
- Dismiss your accomplishments while magnifying your flaws.
- Push through pain instead of resting or asking for help.
- Say yes to everyone else but never to yourself.
- Ignore your intuition because you don't trust your own judgment.
- Feel guilty any time you set a boundary.
- Keep promises to others—but always break the ones you make to yourself.

This list isn't here to shame you. It's here to help you see, maybe for the first time, that your relationship with yourself *matters*. The way you talk to yourself, care for yourself, and advocate for yourself sets the tone for every other relationship in your life.

I know what it's like to live in that toxic space. I didn't just criticize myself—I accepted that same treatment from others because I thought that's what I deserved. When you spend enough time breaking your own trust, you stop expecting anything better.

You don't build unshakeable confidence by being perfect. You build it by telling the truth, especially to yourself.

And sometimes the truth is this: You've failed to treat yourself well. You've ignored what you needed. You've tolerated things you shouldn't have from others *and* from yourself. You've broken your own trust. But none of that makes you broken. It makes you human.

When I think about my relationship with myself during my time with John, I don't just see a lack of confidence; I see a long list of quiet failures. Failing to rest. Failing to speak up. Failing to believe I deserved better. But looking back, I don't see those failures as proof that I was weak. Instead, I see them as signs that I was trying to survive with the tools I had.

And that's the shift. This isn't about shaming yourself into change. It's about recognizing where you've been and choosing to write a different story moving forward. Because the story you tell yourself becomes the life you live.

You can't walk away from yourself, but you *can* stop treating yourself like the enemy. You can choose a different relationship with the person who matters most. You.

LET GO OF THE TOXIC RELATIONSHIP YOU HAVE WITH YOURSELF

Letting go of a toxic relationship with yourself doesn't mean pretending it never existed. It means making a choice, sometimes daily, to stop feeding the patterns that keep you stuck in self-sabotage and shame. Tell yourself a better story. And then live it.

A toxic self-relationship often mirrors what we've tolerated from others. In fact, one of the reasons we stay in toxic relationships with other people is because we've gotten used to treating ourselves the same way. That kind of criticism, neglect, and boundary breaking feels familiar. Safe, even. But it's not. It's damaging, and it bleeds into everything.

Before Vincent van Gogh ever picked up a paintbrush, he admired a successful painter named Jules Breton. At the time, van Gogh wasn't an artist—he was working as a missionary in a struggling coal-mining town in Belgium. But something in him wanted more. So, he made a decision: He was going to walk to Breton's hometown. Nearly fifty miles on foot. Why? Maybe it was admiration. Maybe curiosity. Maybe a quiet hope that someone he respected might see something in him.

But when he got there, he didn't knock on the door. He was too intimidated, so he turned around and walked all the way back.[54]

No one there rejected him ... but he had already rejected himself.

That's what self-sabotage can look like. Not loud. Not dramatic. Just one quiet moment where you decide not to try. Where you tell yourself, *I'm not ready* or *I don't belong.* And you walk away from something you might have been made for.

That's the kind of toxic relationship with ourselves that often goes unnoticed. No one else sees it. But inside, we are constantly talking ourselves out of the very things we want most—not because we're lazy or broken, but because fear has been living rent-free in our minds for so long that it starts to sound like the truth.

But just like van Gogh, our missed moments don't define us. They can wake us up. They can show us where we've been holding ourselves back and help us choose differently next time.

That's why the way we treat ourselves matters so much.

When you constantly talk down to yourself, ignore your limits, or break promises you make to yourself, you're teaching your brain that your needs don't matter. That your voice doesn't count. That you're not worth protecting.

If you don't believe you matter, it becomes almost impossible to expect others to treat you like you do.

This is why it's so important to stop the cycle. To stop waiting for something bad to happen. To stop treating yourself like a problem to fix or a punishment to endure. That mindset isn't just unhealthy—it's exhausting. And it's not who you are.

You were never meant to survive on criticism and chaos. You were meant to thrive with compassion and confidence. Stop treating yourself like a problem to fix. Start treating yourself like someone worth loving.

Stop treating yourself like a problem to fix. Start treating yourself like someone worth loving.

Letting go of the toxic relationship with yourself starts by naming it for what it is and then choosing something better. It doesn't happen overnight. But with each choice to rest instead of push, to speak kindly instead of harshly, to listen to your intuition instead of silencing it, you start to rebuild something sacred.

You begin to believe, maybe for the first time, that you're worth receiving love—especially from yourself.

REBUILDING TRUST WITH YOURSELF

I remember standing in front of the mirror after I left John, looking myself in the eye and making a vow I thought I'd never break. Never again. Never again will I let someone treat me like that.

But here's the part I didn't understand back then: Just because I had left him didn't mean I'd left the damage behind.

Even years later—after I had moved on, built a beautiful life, had a family, and grown into a strong and capable woman—I still heard echoes of his voice. Only this time, it wasn't him. It was me. I was the one picking myself apart. I was the one questioning my worth, tearing myself down for not being perfect, not doing enough, not being enough.

I had walked away from the relationship, but I was still trapped in the mindset it left behind. And the hardest part was that I didn't even realize I was doing it. It felt normal. Familiar. Like this was just how life worked. Like confidence was something other people had, but I was always chasing.

That's when I realized something huge: The promise I made in the mirror wasn't really about John. It was about me. And if I was going to heal, I had to stop *waiting* for me to start treating myself better—and finally do it.

Rebuilding trust with yourself takes time. It means showing up when you say you will. It means being honest about your needs and boundaries—and respecting them. It means being kind to yourself when you mess up. It means choosing yourself, even when it's hard, even when you're scared, even when you don't feel like you deserve it yet.

This isn't about perfection. It's about partnership—with yourself. You are in a relationship with the woman in the mirror, and just like any other relationship, it needs nurturing, patience, and honesty to grow strong.

And here's the truth that shifted my perspective: You don't rebuild trust through a single grand gesture. You rebuild it through daily decisions and quiet, consistent actions that say: You matter. I've got you. I'm not going anywhere.

SO, WHAT DO YOU DO?

Once you realize you've been in a toxic relationship with yourself, you might feel overwhelmed. You might wonder, *How do I even begin to change something that's been part of me for so long?*

The answer isn't to overhaul your life overnight. It's to start small—really small—and build trust with yourself one decision at a time.

Here are five ways to begin:

1. **When you make a promise to yourself, keep it.** If you say you're going to do something—whether it's going for a walk, saying no, or going to bed earlier—honor that. Not to be productive. Not to earn anything. But because you matter.
2. **Talk to yourself like you would your best friend.** Start by noticing your inner dialogue. Would you say that to your child? To your best friend? If not, pause and rephrase.
3. **Set one boundary and hold it.** Boundaries aren't selfish; they're how you protect your peace. Start with one. It could be as simple as turning off your phone at a certain time or saying no without overexplaining.
4. **Celebrate small wins.** Confidence doesn't come from doing big things perfectly. It comes from noticing when you follow through, even a little, and saying, Look at me. I did that.

5. **Offer yourself grace.**
   You're going to mess up. That's part of growth. When you do, practice forgiving yourself with compassion rather than criticism.

You don't need a massive breakthrough to change your life. You just need a series of quiet moments where you decide to treat yourself better than you did yesterday.

This is how you shift the relationship. This is how you rebuild trust. And this—*this*—is how confidence flourishes.

LET GO OF THE PAST AND EMBRACE WHAT IS

Healing starts with how you choose to see yourself and what you choose to carry.

One thing I'm constantly saying to my kids is: "What's in the past is in the past. Learn from it and move forward." And honestly, I need that reminder just as much as they do. Because the truth is, we all mess up. We all fall short. But what we did (or didn't do) yesterday doesn't get to decide who we are today.

The most powerful thing you can do for your future is to stop beating yourself up for the past. It's over. What matters now is how you move forward—with compassion, accountability, and a willingness to believe that you still deserve good things.

Let the past inform you, not define you. Growth happens in the moving forward.

Let the past inform you, not define you. Growth happens in the moving forward.

Start by remembering this: You have 100 percent worth and value every single day. Not because of what you've accomplished, but because you exist. You matter. Period.

View yourself with the same grace you'd offer a friend. What would you say to someone you love who was struggling? Say it to yourself. And keep saying it, especially when it feels hardest to believe.

Be patient with yourself. I know I'm guilty of racing ahead, always trying to get to the next thing before I've even finished the first. But growth takes time. Healing takes time. Confidence takes time. We don't have to rush it. We have to stay with it.

At the same time, hold yourself accountable. If you set a goal, take steps toward it. Surround yourself with people who support you and remind you who you are. That's what my husband and kids do for me. They can't create my confidence, but they help me remember it when I forget.

Above all, speak kindly to yourself. What you say matters. The words you use to describe yourself shape the way you see yourself. If you want to stop living in a toxic relationship with yourself, start by changing the language.

Practice saying good things about yourself, even if they feel awkward or unearned. Confidence isn't something you wait for;

it's something you practice. And the more you practice it, the more real it becomes.

Letting go of the past doesn't mean pretending it never happened. It means not letting it control who you are today. It's choosing to speak to yourself with more compassion and to finally see your strength, your growth, and your worth—clearly and without apology.

Healing from toxic relationships, whether with others or with yourself, isn't a onetime event. It's a series of quiet, powerful choices: setting boundaries, breaking old patterns, telling the truth even when your voice shakes. You don't have to have all the answers. What matters is that you never abandon yourself.

Healing isn't about becoming someone new. It's about coming home to who you've always been.

KEEPING IT REAL

THE SELF-TRUST CHECK-IN

1. Pick one small promise to make to yourself today. It doesn't need to be a massive goal—just something meaningful. A walk. A boundary. Drinking water. Turning off your phone by 9:00 p.m.
2. Write it down:
   Today, I promise myself I will ___________________."
3. Follow through—no excuses, no guilt. Not to be productive. Not to prove anything. Just to rebuild the relationship you have with yourself.
4. Then check in at the end of the day:
   - Did I follow through? ______________________
   - How did that feel?

     ____

     ____

     ____

   - What did that small act of self-respect teach me?

     ____

     ____

     ____

PILLAR #2 EXERCISES

EMBRACE YOUR FAILURES

If you truly want to learn how to embrace your failures, it's time to put your learning into practice. Here are ten different exercises to help build your confidence by embracing your failures. Choose one of these exercises and follow through with it. You can come back and choose a different exercise as often as you need to. Remember—the courage to grow comes from your willingness to try, so don't skip these exercises. They are an important part of building REAL confidence.

1. FAILURE LOGBOOK

Each time you feel you've "failed" at something, write it down in a dedicated logbook. Reflect on what you learned from the experience and how it helped you grow. For example:

- Failure: "I didn't meet my work deadline."
- Growth: "I learned to communicate better with my team and set realistic timelines."

2. TINY COURAGE CHALLENGES

Make a list of several small actions that feel uncomfortable but aren't overwhelming (e.g., speaking up in a meeting or

trying a new hobby). Commit to doing one of these "tiny courage challenges" each day for a week.

Afterward, write down how you felt, regardless of the outcome, and note any growth from trying.

3. WHAT'S THE WORST THAT COULD HAPPEN?

Think of something you're afraid to try because of a fear of failure. Write down the worst-case scenario and then brainstorm solutions to handle it. This exercise helps reduce the fear of failure by preparing you to face potential setbacks.

4. GROWTH REFLECTION JOURNAL

At the end of each day, write about one way you demonstrated the courage to try something new or challenging. Reflect on what you learned, even if things didn't go as planned. For example, you might write, "I tried a new workout routine. I didn't complete it, but I discovered I enjoy yoga."

5. FAILURE REFRAME

Write down a past failure that still feels significant to you. Reframe it by listing at least three positive outcomes or lessons you gained from that experience. For example:

- Failure: "I didn't get the job I wanted."
- Growth: "I gained interview experience, learned to tailor my resume, and found an even better opportunity later."
- Failure:

  ____

- Growth:

  ____

  ____

  ____

6. COURAGE VISUALIZATION

Close your eyes and imagine yourself taking a bold step toward something you've been avoiding. Visualize what it feels like to try, even if you don't succeed. Focus on the feeling of courage and growth rather than the outcome.

7. FAILURE STORYTELLING

Share a personal story of failure with a trusted friend or family member, or write it down in a journal. Highlight what you learned and how the experience helped you grow. This practice builds resilience and normalizes failure as part of growth.

8. TRY TO CELEBRATE

Pick something new you've been hesitant to try. After attempting it, celebrate your effort—not the result. For example: "I tried public speaking for the first time. It wasn't perfect, but I'm proud I had the courage to do it."

9. FAILURE AFFIRMATIONS

Create affirmations that embrace failure as part of growth, such as:

- "Every failure is a step toward my success."
- "I have the courage to try, and that's what matters."

Repeat these affirmations daily or when facing challenges.

10. THE GROWTH MINDSET JAR

Fill a jar with notes each time you try something new or face a failure with courage. Write what you learned or how it contributed to your growth. Over time, the jar becomes a physical reminder of your progress and resilience.

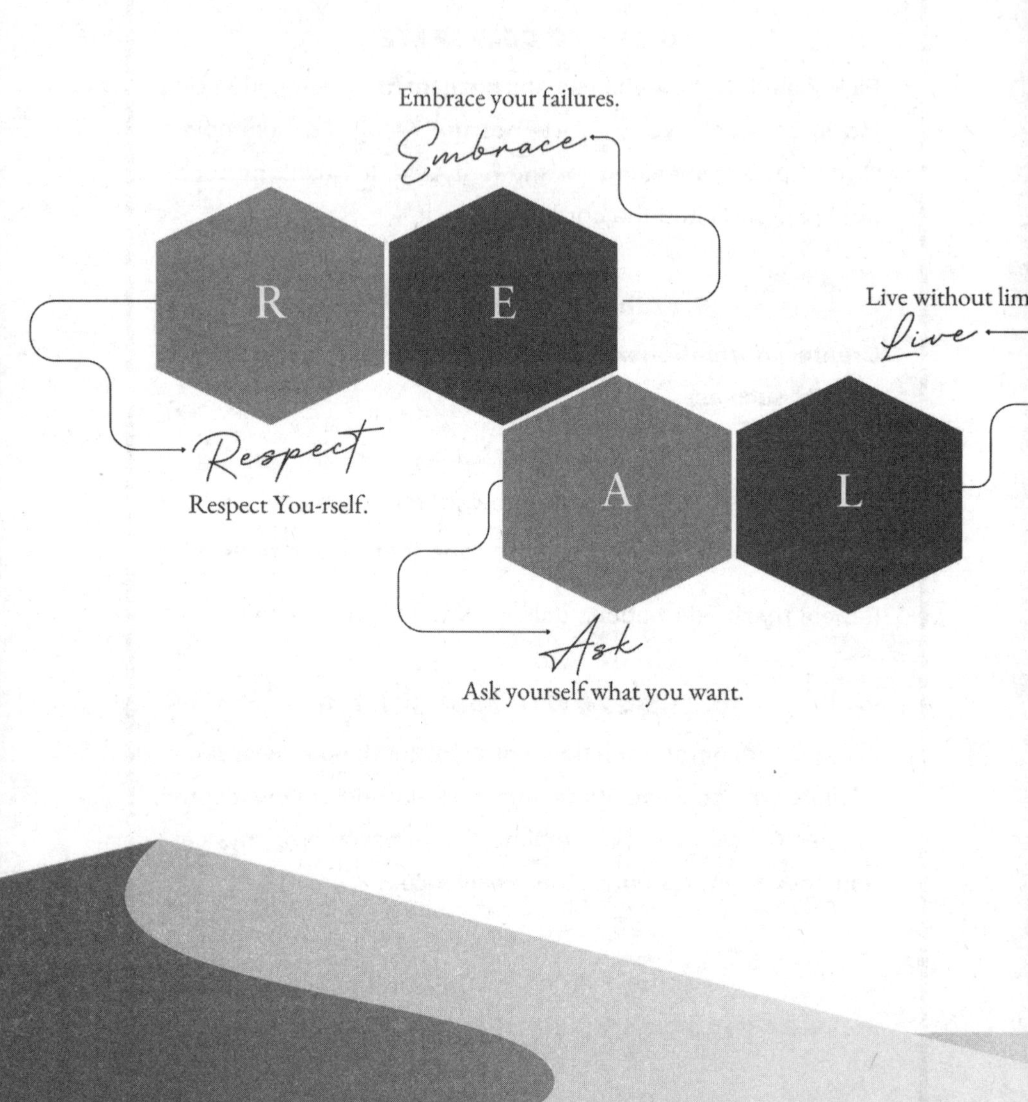
Embrace your failures.
Embrace
R
E
Live without lim
Live
Respect
Respect You-rself.
A
L
Ask
Ask yourself what you want.

PILLAR #3

ASK YOURSELF WHAT YOU WANT

Asking yourself what you truly want is a powerful act of self-awareness and intention. It's not just about setting goals; it's about aligning your desires with your values and purpose. Discovering what you want creates space for who you're meant to be, allowing you to step into a life of clarity and fulfillment. When you take the time to reflect on your dreams and ambitions, you begin to shed the expectations of others and focus on what truly matters to you. This clarity ignites a path forward, empowering you to take action with confidence and live authentically.

Chapter Eight

THE POWER OF KNOWING WHAT YOU WANT

"Decide what you want. Believe you can have it. Believe you deserve it. And believe it's possible for you."[55]

RHONDA BYRNE

Have you ever asked yourself what you really want out of life?

I mean really asked—without filtering it through what your family needs, what your job expects, or what the world says you *should* want?

If you're like me, it's probably been a while.

The truth is, we get so caught up in the chaos of everyday life that we stop asking ourselves that simple yet essential question. We're busy taking care of everyone else, and somewhere along the way, our own dreams get buried under laundry piles, calendar reminders, and late-night to-do lists.

For a long time, I didn't ask myself what I wanted either. I told myself that if everyone else was happy, then I was doing something right. That my needs could wait. That it was selfish to want more.

But here's the thing: That way of thinking never worked.

Everyone else might have been happy—but I wasn't. I felt disconnected, stuck, and honestly … a little invisible. When you stop asking yourself what you want, you slowly start to lose the confidence to go after it. Clarity starts the moment you tell yourself the truth.

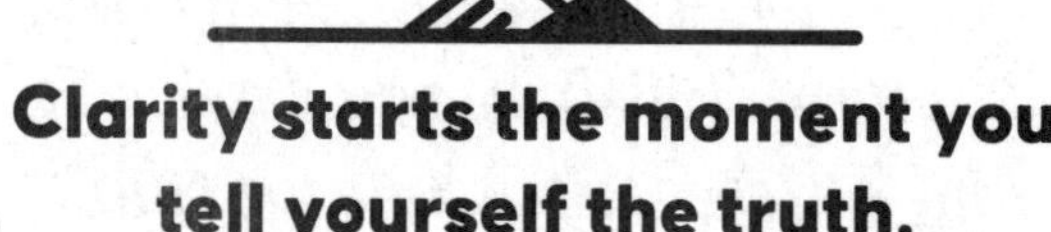

Clarity starts the moment you tell yourself the truth.

FOR YEARS I LIVED WITH SELF-DOUBT

As I mentioned earlier, even though I've always had a supportive family and great parents, self-doubt has been a constant companion. I have an incredible husband who's always in my corner. I have children who cheer me on. But for the longest time, I still felt like I wasn't enough. It wasn't because of them; it was because of me.

Somewhere in the busyness of everyday life, I forgot who I was. I became Rob's wife. My children's mom. The cook, the chauffeur, the one holding it all together. And while I deeply value those roles, I lost sight of the fact that I was more than "just" the person making sure everyone else was okay.

Even though Rob always supported whatever I wanted to do, the problem was that I didn't really know *what* I wanted to do. For the first forty years of my life, I did the things I thought I was supposed to do, and I did those things simply because that's what I thought I was supposed to be doing.

Now, don't get me wrong, I love being a wife and a mother. I still did fun things along the way. It's not that I didn't do anything for myself.

But I never really asked myself the question, *What do I want?*

CLIMBING MOUNT KILIMANJARO CHANGED MY LIFE

In 2015, something shifted for me. You've already heard my Kilimanjaro story, but here's what I didn't realize at the time: When I said yes to the climb, I wasn't just saying yes to a mountain. I was saying yes to me. To growth. To clarity. To possibility.

I was asked if I wanted to climb Mount Kilimanjaro, and without even thinking it through, I said yes. Who does that?

Looking back, I'm not even sure why I said yes so quickly. Maybe it was because I was so used to meeting other people's expectations that I didn't know how to say no. Maybe it was because I didn't want to disappoint anyone. Or maybe, deep down, I knew I needed something that would shake me out of the routine I'd been living in for so long.

Whatever the reason, I said yes. And that one word changed everything.

I live in Florida. Climbing any kind of mountain was completely out of my wheelhouse. But I needed to get out of my comfort zone. I needed to see what I was capable of.

Once I committed, I realized I had a lot of work to do—not just physically, but mentally too. The altitude and terrain were certainly big obstacles, but they weren't the biggest challenges. The real challenge was about whether I believed in myself enough to keep putting one foot in front of the other.

It was the first time I'd ever set a goal like this, trained for it, and followed through. And maybe more importantly, it was the first time I truly trusted myself enough to even try.

I traveled with complete strangers. My tentmate was someone I'd never met before the trip. But she turned out to be one of the most positive, grounded people I've ever known. We pushed each other, supported each other, and laughed through the exhaustion.

I went up that mountain with strangers and came down with lifelong friends.

But more than that, I came down with a version of myself I hadn't seen in years.

When I said yes to the climb, I didn't realize I was also saying yes to *me*. To growth. To clarity. To possibility.

I didn't just climb a mountain. I found myself again.

I hadn't even realized I was lost. Say one small brave yes this week. Action creates clarity.

Say one small brave yes this week. Action creates clarity.

THE MOMENT I FOUND MYSELF

Despite the altitude, the exhaustion, and every single voice in my head that told me I couldn't—I made it.

I stood at the summit of Mount Kilimanjaro, and I just … breathed. The air was thin, the wind was sharp, and my legs were shaking. But I was there.

The girl who once questioned everything about herself.

The girl who had been mentally and physically abused as a teenager.

The girl who spent years second-guessing her worth, wondering if she was enough.

That girl was standing on top of the tallest mountain in Africa.

And in that moment, I didn't feel small. I didn't feel uncertain. I felt strong. Clear. Present.

I stood still for a while, letting tears come up from a place deep in my heart. I felt a release, a quiet realization that all those old stories I used to tell myself—*you're not strong enough, you're not capable, you're not worthy*—they just weren't true anymore.

Because I had done something I never thought I could do.

That changed something in me.

This was the moment I found myself—not in some big, cinematic way, but in the kind of way that stays with you.

A deep knowing. A steady, grounded truth. Like I'd finally come home to myself.

It didn't flip a switch overnight. Confidence like that doesn't show up all at once. But this climb was a turning point. It was a moment I can trace everything else back to.

I didn't just climb a mountain that day.

I climbed over self-doubt. I climbed into belief. I climbed into trust.

And I came down knowing I would never see myself the same way again.

LIFE IS ALL ABOUT CHOICES

Climbing Mount Kilimanjaro helped me realize something simple but powerful: Everything from our past leads us to this very moment. Every choice we've made, every mountain we've climbed, literal or not, has brought us here.

And while we've all had our fair share of challenges, those hard moments have shaped us. They've made us who we are.

I'm sure you've faced your own. Maybe you're even going through something difficult right now. If that's the case, I see you. I don't want to downplay what you're going through or pretend it's easy. But here's what I've come to believe: No matter what life throws at us, we always have a choice in how we respond.

Every morning we wake up, we get to choose. Every day, we're faced with small decisions that shape our lives in big ways. We get to decide who we want to be and how we want to show up.

Once we've made that decision, our actions bring it to life. And those actions don't have to be big. In fact, most of the time, they shouldn't be.

When I was climbing Kilimanjaro, the guides would repeat a Swahili phrase over and over: *pole pole* (pronounced *po-lay po-lay*). It means "slowly, slowly." It was a reminder to pace ourselves, not just physically, but mentally and emotionally too. To be present. To breathe. To keep going, one step at a time. That same idea applies to life. You don't have to move fast to move forward. You just have to keep showing up.

We often think we need to wait for the "right" time, like New Year's Day or Monday morning. We don't.

You don't need a fresh start on the calendar to make a new choice. You need a moment of clarity and the willingness to take the first step. If something in your life isn't working, you can change it. You don't have to overhaul everything at once—but you can make a new choice, and then follow it with one small action. And then another.

Pole pole.

Choice leads to action.

Action builds confidence.

Confidence opens doors.

And the best part is that you get to choose yourself again every day.

IT'S OKAY TO CHANGE YOUR MIND

Most of us grow up thinking that once we pick a profession, we're stuck with it for life.

Sadly, that mindset begins way too young. We expect teenagers to know what they want to do with the rest of their lives before they even finish growing up. Whether it's college or something else, by the time you're eighteen, there's this pressure to choose your path—and then to stick to it.

So, we do our best. We pick something. We try to follow through. And then we stay in it . . . even when it no longer fits. Even when we've outgrown it. Even when it slowly starts to steal our joy.

It's like we don't realize that it's okay to change your mind.

Now, I'm not saying you should go out and quit your job tomorrow. We all have responsibilities, and sometimes the job we're in is what supports us or our families. But what I *am* saying is that you need to give yourself permission to start asking the question: *Is this still what I want?*

It took me until my late forties to find the thing I love most—and it didn't happen until I finally allowed myself to be curious again.

We're not meant to stay the same forever. You're not the same person you were at eighteen or even twenty-eight. Life has changed you. Experiences have shaped you. And it's only natural for your goals and passions to evolve too.

A new perspective can lead to a new direction, and there's nothing wrong with that.

So no, you don't have to burn everything down. But you *can* start paying attention to that quiet pull that tells you there's something more.

Because sometimes, all it takes is one honest question to start building a life that feels more aligned, more joyful—and more *you*.

And that question is simple:

What do I want?

WHAT DO YOU ACTUALLY WANT?

This question might feel uncomfortable at first, but ask it anyway.

What do I actually want?

It's such a simple question, but for so many of us, the answer is buried. Buried under obligations, responsibilities, expectations ... maybe even self-doubt.

Try to think back to what you wanted when you were a kid. Before fear or practicality took over. Before someone told you to be "realistic." Remember that version of yourself? The one who believed anything was possible?

That version of you still exists.

So much of adulthood is about figuring out what's expected of us. But what if we paused long enough to ask what *we* expect of life?

One of my favorite questions to ask is, *What would you do if there were no limits?* No fear, no pressure, no one to impress—just you, your values, and a blank canvas.

What makes you happy?

What fills you up?

What gives your life meaning?

Those aren't throwaway questions; they're your compass. They'll guide you toward something real.

And if you're still feeling stuck, here's another way in:

What don't you want?

Sometimes it's easier to spot what's no longer working than to name what you're reaching for:

- What have you outgrown?
- What feels heavy, draining, or misaligned?
- What are you tolerating that you'd never want someone you love to settle for?

Getting honest about what no longer fits creates room for what *does*.

We get so used to tolerating things—relationships, roles, and routines—that we forget we're allowed to let go of what drains us. Getting honest about what you *don't* want can clear the space for what you do.

Once you start asking honest questions, it gets easier to hear honest answers.

And once you know what you want—really want—the next question is this:

Am I willing to do the work to make it happen?

You probably haven't heard of Vicki Anstey, but her story might just change the way you think about confidence. At thirty-nine, she walked away from a controlling marriage and a career that no longer fit. She didn't have a plan—just a glimpse of herself in the mirror one day that made her realize she was tired of living small.

So, she started simple: a fitness class here, a tough conversation there. Then she kept going. She became a finalist on the reality show *SAS: Who Dares Wins* (2019). She rowed across the Pacific—despite a fear of water. She cycled three thousand miles across America. She broke two world records.[56]

She did all this, not because she felt confident, but because she was willing to do the work anyway.

Nothing changes unless you do. Confidence comes from choosing, not wishing. Choosing to act. Choosing to show up. Choosing to go for it, even if the road feels uncertain.

So, ask the questions.

Listen to the answers.

And when you're ready, go after what you want with everything you've got.

Because you're allowed to want more.

You're allowed to want different.

And you are absolutely capable of making it happen.

DON'T LET OTHER PEOPLE DETERMINE YOUR DESTINY

When you're trying to figure out what you really want, it's easy to let other people's voices drown out your own.

People love to share their opinions, especially when you haven't asked for them. And they'll often speak with full confidence, even when they have no idea what's actually right for you. But you don't have to take someone's advice just because they offer it.

It's your life. Your story. Your future. No one else gets to write it for you.

When I got engaged to Rob, I was just twenty years old—and he was ten years older than me. People had *a lot* to say about that.

"Are you sure you're ready?"

"He's so much older!"

"Do you really think your marriage is going to last?"

But I knew what I wanted. And more importantly, I knew who Rob was, and I trusted that. Thirty-two years later, we're still here. Still growing. Still proving that love isn't defined by age, but by commitment, communication, and shared values.

Then came Mount Kilimanjaro.

"Wait—you're climbing *what*?"

"You know that's a serious mountain, right?"

"Do you really think you'll make it to the top?"

It's wild how quickly people will project their fears onto your dreams.

No one walks down the aisle thinking their marriage is going to fail. And no one commits to climbing a mountain thinking they'll only go halfway. I didn't need anyone else's permission to take that leap, and I certainly didn't need their doubt.

People will always have something to say. They'll question your timing, your capacity, your decisions. Sometimes it comes from love, sometimes from fear—but either way, you don't have to internalize it.

I spent far too many years letting other people's opinions influence what I wore, where I went, what I said yes or no to. Until one day, I realized I was living more for their comfort than my own joy.

And I decided to stop.

If I'm living with integrity, if I'm showing up with love, if I feel good about the choices I'm making, then someone else's discomfort doesn't get to steer the ship.

Neither does their doubt.

You get to choose what matters to you. You get to choose the life you want to live. Don't let someone else's fear or judgment talk you out of it.

You don't have to explain your dreams to anyone.

You have to be brave enough to chase them.

WHAT'S HOLDING YOU BACK?

Sometimes we want to move forward, but something invisible keeps pulling us back.

If that sounds familiar, I want to offer you a few questions. I only ask that you answer them with complete honesty:

- What's holding you back? (Really sit with that for a minute.)
- What's keeping you from finding your Kilimanjaro?
- Are you happy where you are right now?
- Do you want something to change?

- Are you so busy living up to everyone else's expectations that you've forgotten who you really are?
- Have you lost touch with the little kid who once dreamed big—of being an astronaut, a rock star, a teacher, a storyteller?

That last question still gets me, because that child is still in there, still dreaming, still waiting. Do you remember what you used to say when people asked what you wanted to be when you grew up? Are you anywhere near that dream?

When I was little, I wanted to be an actress. I've shared this before, but it's relevant here too because it shows how early I started trading my own dreams for what others thought was practical. And I carried that pattern with me for years.

And yet, here I am.

I write.

I speak on stages.

I tell stories.

I host a podcast.

I connect with people in a way that feels *so right.*

In a way, I guess I *am* doing what I always dreamed of. I just had to take the scenic route to get here.

Coming back to what I really wanted, and actually living it, has made my life feel more beautiful than I ever imagined.

And I'm more confident than ever … because I'm doing exactly what I was meant to do.

But this isn't about me. It's about you.

Because maybe there's a version of *your* dream that got buried under someone else's expectations. Maybe you've taken detours, hit dead ends, or convinced yourself it's too late to want something different.

But it's not too late. You can still come back to what you really want. You can still listen to that younger version of yourself, the one who dreamed without limits, and choose to start now.

Confidence doesn't come from having it all figured out. It comes from being honest about what you want … and being brave enough to go after it.

So, let me ask you again: What do you actually want? And what's one small step you can take today to move toward it?

AN EASY COMPASS TO GUIDE YOU

If you're still feeling unsure about what you really want or are struggling to make a decision with confidence, I have a process that's helped me more times than I can count.

I call it my *Compass Check-In Method.*

When I'm at a crossroads, I ask myself these four questions:

1. *Does this feel like it aligns with who I am right now?*
2. *Will this add to my well-being or drain it?*
3. *Am I doing this out of love or out of guilt?*
4. *Does this move me closer to the life I actually want?*

These questions act like a compass. They help point me toward what feels right—not just what looks right on paper.

What if the answer to most of those questions is *no*? That's my signal to pause and reevaluate.

Of course, life isn't black and white. There will be times when we make compromises. (Like when I go to an amusement park: I don't exactly feel *nourished*, but my kids are thrilled, and that matters too.) But if you're *always* the one compromising or if you're constantly pushing aside your needs to keep the peace or meet someone else's expectations, it might be time to check your compass.

Confidence doesn't come from following someone else's map.

It comes from tuning into your own internal guide and trusting where it's leading you.

I remember using my Compass Check-In Method during my time in medical sales. On paper, it looked like the perfect job with steady income, a flexible schedule, and plenty of room to grow. But the reality was different. Over time, I started to feel uneasy about what the role was becoming.

I was constantly asked, "What can you give me?" And in medical sales, that's not just unethical—it's illegal. Some doctors even suggested I offer gift cards, saying those didn't really count as compensation. But I said no. Every time. I refused to cross that line.

That experience showed me it wasn't just about sales; it was about integrity. And mine wasn't up for negotiation. Saying no wasn't easy, but it reminded me of who I am and what I stand for. It also made something clear: I wanted to do work that aligned with my values, work that allowed me to make a real impact without compromising what mattered most.

That realization became the turning point that led me toward something bigger and far more meaningful.

Sometimes, before we can move toward what we really want, we need to pause and check in with ourselves. That's what the Compass Check-In helps us do—it grounds us in the present. It gives us clarity when we feel stuck or unsure.

But once you've taken that pause and gotten honest about what's working and what's not, the next step is to look ahead.

This is where *dreaming forward* matters.

Because knowing what you want is one thing. Daring to say it out loud—and to take steps toward it—that's something else entirely.

DARE TO DREAM

We all have dreams tucked inside us—some we've carried since childhood, and others we've only recently begun to recognize. But sometimes, we just need a gentle nudge to take them seriously and start moving toward them.

I created the **DREAM Framework** to help you get clear on what you want and take that first step toward it. Here's how it works:

Grab a journal or a piece of paper and a pen, and walk through this with me. Don't overthink it. Just write what comes up.

Let this be a moment for *you*.

The DREAM Framework: Reflect and Pursue

D — Discover

- Take time to uncover what truly excites and fulfills you. Explore your passions and curiosities—without judgment.
- Question: What makes you feel alive and inspired?

R — Reflect

- Think about why this dream matters to you. How does it connect to your values and who you are?
- Question: Why is this important to me, and what does it reveal about what I care most about?

E — Envision

- Picture it. Really see it. Imagine your life with that dream realized.
- Question: What does my dream life look and feel like?

A — Align

- Make sure your dream fits with your authentic self—your strengths, your season of life, and your values.
- Question: How does this dream align with who I am and where I want to go?

M — Manifest

- Bring it to life. Start small. Stay consistent. Believe in it enough to take action, even if it's just one step today.
- Question: What's one thing I can do today to move this dream forward?

My hope is that you use the DREAM Framework not just to think about your dreams but to *chase* them. The only thing standing between you and your dream might be the courage to say yes to it.

GIVE YOURSELF PERMISSION

Some people seem to have life all figured out. They love what they do, and they've done it forever.

The majority of us, however, definitely do not have everything figured out, and we don't give ourselves permission to pursue our dreams. We think we need a perfect plan or clear direction before we begin, but sometimes clarity only comes through action.

Take Rob Lawless, for example. After leaving a traditional consulting job, he started Project 10,000 Friends, an ambitious goal to have ten thousand one-hour conversations with strangers.[57] No script. No strategy. Just connection. What he learned after thousands of conversations is something we all need to hear: most people don't have it all figured out. They're just doing the best they can, asking questions, trying things, and learning along the way. And the ones who seem the most confident? They're the ones who gave themselves permission to start, even without all the answers. Permission is the doorway. Action is the proof.

Permission is the doorway. Action is the proof.

If this is you, the best way to figure out what you actually want is to start asking yourself questions that you've probably never asked yourself before:

- Is this the relationship that you want?
- Is this the profession that you want?
- Is this the family life that you want?
- Above all, what do you want?

I am in no way saying that you should leave any of these things behind. However, there is a way to make positive change in every aspect of your life by simply giving yourself permission to ask yourself these questions.

If your relationship is struggling, ask yourself what you want in a relationship, and then put in the work to get it.

If your family life is less than ideal, ask yourself what it would look like if you set a goal and put in the work to make a positive change.

You may not have the perfect life (no one does), but you can have an *exceptional* life if you are willing to ask yourself what it is you want and then do the work to make it happen.

Stop accepting things as they are and put in the work to make them what they could be. Give yourself permission to get outside your comfort zone and be the champion of your own change. Give yourself permission to ignore the naysayers and become the architect of your own life. Give yourself permission to be seen and heard exactly as you are. Above all, give yourself permission to figure out what it is that you really, truly want, then go out there and get it. It's always been there waiting for you.

REAL confidence comes when you're willing to ask yourself the hard questions and then give yourself permission to follow wherever those answers lead. The answers are there, just waiting for you to discover them.

So, get to work and make it happen.

KEEPING IT REAL

DARE TO DREAM

You've just spent time exploring what it means to ask yourself what you really want—and now it's time to take action.

Earlier in this chapter, I shared my **DREAM Framework** to help you reflect, align, and move forward with clarity. If you haven't already, take a moment to walk through that process. Then, come back here and try this:

Grab your journal or a piece of paper and respond to the questions below—not with what sounds good, but with what feels true.

1. What lights you up inside—even if it doesn't make sense to anyone else?
   (This is often where your dream begins.)

   ____

   ____

   ____

2. What are you holding on to that no longer serves you?
   (A thought, a habit, a belief? Be honest—it's okay to let it go.)

   ____

3. **If you could rewrite one part of your current life, what would you change?**
   (One thing. Big or small.)

4. **Where do you feel most like you—and how can you make space for more of that?**
   (This is where alignment lives.)

5. **What's one step—just one—you can take this week to move closer to the life you actually want?**

Chapter Nine

CALM YOUR FEARS

"The thing you fear most has no power. Your fear of it is what has the power. Facing the truth really will set you free."[58]

OPRAH WINFREY

Once you know what you want, there's usually one thing standing between you and actually going after it: fear.

Fear is tricky. It's layered. It's loud. And it's not always the villain.

Some fear is healthy. It's your body's way of keeping you safe—your built-in alarm system that says, *Hey, maybe don't run into traffic. Maybe don't pet the alligator.* That kind of fear serves a purpose. It's there to protect you.

But then there's the other kind. The kind that whispers, *You're not good enough.* The kind that convinces you to stay small, stay silent, or stay stuck. The kind that stops you from even trying—just in case you might fail.

That's the kind of fear that doesn't protect you.

It holds you back.

FEAR WAS MY CONSTANT COMPANION

When I was younger, fear ran the show.

For me, it was fear of failure and fear of judgment. Both worked overtime in my mind, shaping my decisions, holding me back, and convincing me I had to be perfect in order to be accepted.

I didn't talk about it, not even with my husband, Rob. Not because I couldn't, but because I was afraid of what it would mean to say the words out loud. I thought that acknowledging the fear would make it real, and then it would take over. So, I held it in and kept moving. I told myself I had to be the strong one—for the kids, for Rob, for everyone. But the truth is, no one else was asking that of me. I was the one who decided I wasn't allowed to fall apart. I thought if I let even one crack show, everything would break wide open. So I stayed quiet, and I let fear do the talking.

When people asked how I was doing, I'd smile and say, "I'm fine."

You know—that version of "fine" that really means freaked out, insecure, neurotic, and emotional. The kind of fine where you smile in the school pickup line, but your eye is twitching, and you've been reheating the same cup of coffee since 8:00 a.m. You're holding it together with dry shampoo, caffeine, and a whole lot of pretending. That kind of fine.

I wanted to feel the way people saw me. Strong. Capable. Unshakeable. I leaned into that image and buried everything else. I figured if I kept showing up like I had it all together, eventually I'd feel that way too.

But fear has a way of catching up to you, especially when you're running on empty. Fear loses power the moment you name it out loud.

Fear loses power the moment you name it out loud.

For me, that moment came years ago, when we had our first three kids. We were heading to Italy, and the timing wasn't great. Our then youngest daughter, Olivia, only three at the time, had just been discharged from the hospital after a tough case of rotavirus. I'd spent the past three nights sleeping in one of those hospital recliners that were definitely not designed for rest. We literally left the hospital and went straight to the airport.

The entire flight, I was locked in on Olivia, checking her temperature, feeding her ice chips, watching her every move like a hawk. I didn't even register what was happening with Jacob. To this day, I'm still not sure if he stayed up the whole time, watched five movies, or ordered ten Diet Cokes from the flight attendant.

And Emma? No idea what she did during the flight. Honestly, I couldn't have told you whether she was watching a movie, sleeping, or doing a handstand in her seat for eight hours. Mom of the year award, right?

We landed in Rome and did what every tired family does: We tried to power through the day and adjust to the time zone. By 7:00 p.m., we all crashed. A few hours later, I woke up to the sound of one of the kids stirring. I was ready to roll over and give a half-asleep "Go back to bed," until I realized something was wrong.

Jacob wasn't just fidgeting. His body was jerking. His eyes rolled back into his head. His limbs were locked stiff as a board. He was having a seizure. It was completely out of the blue. He'd never had one before. But in that moment, I had no idea why it was happening. I was scared out of my mind.

Everything inside me cracked open.

Rob stayed calm—thankfully—and took Jacob to the hospital in the middle of the night. I stayed back at the hotel with the other kids, completely unraveling. I didn't sleep for days. I hovered over Jacob constantly, afraid to even blink. What if it happened again? What if I missed something?

The doctors couldn't give us an explanation. There was nothing to fix, nothing to prepare for. And even though Jacob never had another seizure, the notknowing made me question myself in a way I'll never forget. I felt like I'd failed. Like I had been so focused on one child, I had neglected another. I let that fear sink in and take over. It was like I'd been holding on to a thread, and that thread finally snapped.

That trip didn't make me question whether I was *happy*; it made me question whether I was *capable*. Was I strong enough? Was I was doing any of it right?

Looking back, I know now that my fear wasn't protecting me during that season. It was controlling me.

It seems wild to me that no one else could see it. On the outside, I looked "fine." I appeared calm, composed, and like I was handling it all in stride. But inside, I was exhausted from trying to keep it all together.

I was fighting with everything I had to be the perfect wife and mother, but the only person who expected perfection from me … was me.

That fear stayed with me for a long time. I let it dictate what I did and didn't do for years. I kept showing up, but I wasn't really present. I was just trying to hold it all together and hoping no one would notice how much I was struggling underneath it all.

DON'T BE AFRAID TO SHARE WHO YOU ARE

For a long time, I thought vulnerability meant weakness. I thought if I let people see how much I was struggling, they'd think I wasn't strong—or worse, that I was failing. So, I did what so many of us do: I put on a smile. I kept showing up. I pretended to be fine, even when I wasn't.

But sometimes, life gives you a moment you didn't see coming. A moment that changes everything.

I was sitting in a room full of around six hundred women. I was sharing a table with some of my closest friends—women I loved and who loved me. But even with all that comfort, I had never talked openly about my struggles. Not about my weight or how much I struggled with body image. Not about the pressure I felt to hold everything together. Not about the quiet overwhelm that seemed to follow me everywhere.

And then a video came on—Colbie Caillat's "Try." If you've seen it, you know the power of it. Women wiping away their makeup. Letting go of the pressure. Stripping off the expectations, layer by layer, until what remained was raw, honest, real.

In a moment I didn't plan for, the words just came out.

I started talking. *Really* talking. About the parts of me I usually kept hidden. The self-doubt. The fear. The exhaustion.

And I cried.

That might not sound like a big deal, but for me, at that time in my life, it was. These days, I cry all the time—at commercials, during movies, even when I'm just overwhelmed with joy or life. But back then, I almost never cried—and definitely not in front of people. But something about saying it out loud, admitting I wasn't "fine," felt like a release.

And no one ran away.

They listened. They nodded. They didn't try to fix it. They just sat with me in it.

In that moment, something shifted.

I didn't feel judged. I didn't feel weak. I felt *seen*. For the first time in a long time, I felt like I didn't have to keep pretending.

That's the gift of honesty. When we speak our truth, especially in safe, supportive spaces, we begin to shed the weight of perfection. We stop performing, and we start healing. Vulnerability doesn't weaken connection—it deepens it.

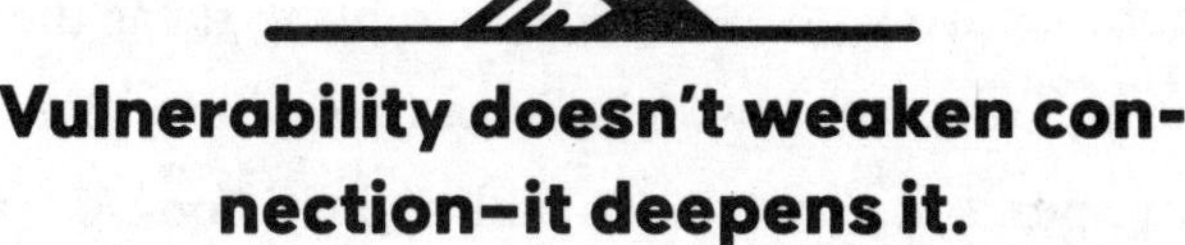

Vulnerability doesn't weaken connection–it deepens it.

Maybe most importantly, we remind each other that we're not alone.

THE POWER OF YOUR MIND

Everyone has something they struggle with. We're all battling something—quiet fears, loud doubts, or invisible stories we tell ourselves on repeat. And most of those battles start in our own minds.

If you truly want to calm your fears, you have to look past the symptoms and dig down to the root of the problem.

In my experience, the kind of fear that holds you back and keeps you stuck usually comes from irrational or exaggerated thoughts. We start imagining worst-case scenarios, jumping to conclusions, or making assumptions that aren't based on actual facts. Then, we tell ourselves stories based on those fears: *I'm not good enough. I'll fail. They'll judge me. I can't do this.*

Fear doesn't always come from reality; it comes from how we interpret it.

That's why managing fear begins with managing your thoughts. Your mind is incredibly powerful. If you want to stop letting fear run the show, the best thing you can do is start noticing and reframing the thoughts that feed it.

You may not realize it, but your own thinking holds so much of the solution. It starts with awareness—simply noticing the thoughts that show up. You can't always control them, but you *can* choose how you respond. And when you shift your response, everything else starts to change.

I learned this in a powerful way from my friend Chris Irwin. Chris knows a thing or two about fear and what it takes to face it. His story changed the way I think about the mind, and it's one I'll never forget.

TOP GUN

Chris Irwin was part of the Top Gun generation. Like so many others, he saw the movie and instantly knew—*that's it.* Fighter pilot. That was the dream.

And he didn't just dream it—he went after it. Chris became the first person in over a decade from his high school to earn an appointment to the Naval Academy. From there, he went on to get his master's degree in international relations from Cambridge.

But while at the Naval Academy, something else caught his attention: the Navy SEALs. To everyone there, they were the superheroes. The elite of the elite. And Chris? He wanted to be one of them.

So, he made it through SEAL training and then joined their ranks—and served for fourteen years on active duty, followed by six years in the reserves. On paper, it was an extraordinary career. He had reached a level of excellence that few ever experience.

But when he left the military, everything changed.

Chris found himself battling something no training had prepared him for: severe anxiety, PTSD, and a chronic illness that left him physically and emotionally depleted. He went from being the guy who could do anything to the guy who could barely get through the day.

So, he went searching for answers.

He saw dozens of practitioners. Took hundreds of supplements. Read every book. Ran every test. Tried every method he could find—even some of the fringe ones. He spent tens of thousands of dollars trying to get better.

But nothing truly worked until one day, something finally clicked.

Chris realized that the solution wasn't somewhere *out there*—it was inside him. The power to heal, to rebuild, to move forward, it was already his. The key was learning how to use his mind in a different way.

That one shift changed everything.

Today, in his early fifties, Chris has made it his mission to share what he's learned, especially with veterans. He created a model called RARE SENSE™, a mental fitness approach that challenges the idea that people are broken or need to be fixed.

Instead, he teaches that change happens the moment we take responsibility for how we think. That we all have the power to shift our own mindset, and in doing so, we unlock the door to real healing and lasting confidence.

Chris's story is a reminder that while fear may live in our minds, so does our strength.

THE IMPORTANCE OF MENTAL FITNESS

Chris's unique perspective on mental health has been changing lives.

He teaches that just as physical fitness is an important part of life, mental fitness is equally important. Instead of trying to get healthy from a treatment perspective, Chris champions the idea that we can take ownership of our own mental health and begin doing the internal work to fix ourselves.

Just like we have routines for our physical health, it's equally important that we have *mind training* for our mental health. Recognizing the importance of mental fitness has been a real game-changer for many who have found healing through Chris's mental fitness model.

The purpose of sharing Chris's experience is to help you understand what is possible when you use the power of your own mind. Chris faced relentless physical and mental challenges during his time as a Navy SEAL, and he was told he was broken. Yet, when he made the decision to take charge of his own healing by first healing his mind, everything changed for him. If Chris can change the trajectory of his life with mental fitness exercises, so can the rest of us.

Now, I want to be clear—I'm not a therapist or mental health specialist. I'm simply sharing what's helped me and what I've learned from people like Chris who've walked these roads with incredible insight. Everyone's journey is different, and it's always okay to seek professional support when you need it.

My mental fitness routine starts with Mirror Moments in the morning, ends with daily gratitudes at night, and carries through the day as I remind myself to give grace. Gratitudes aren't about big achievements; they're about noticing the small things—a kind word, a quiet moment, even a good cup of coffee. Along with affirmations, they've become anchors that keep my mindset strong and my confidence steady.

There are so many things you can do that will help you keep your mind in a place of positivity and mental wellness, but it will require work on your part. Just like you need to put in the work of exercising to keep your body physically fit, you must also put in the work needed to keep your mind healthy and whole.

If you want to overcome your fears and the negative emotions that are holding you back and stealing your confidence, it's important that you discover your own mind exercises. Then, do these exercises regularly to keep your mind mentally fit and capable of facing whatever life throws your way.

Here are a few to get you started:

- **Mirror Moments:** Begin your day by looking yourself in the eye and saying something kind or encouraging. Even one sentence sets the tone.
- **Daily Gratitudes:** Write down three things you're thankful for before bed. They don't have to be big—small moments count.
- **Positive Affirmations:** Repeat a phrase that grounds you, like "I am enough" or "I can handle this."
- **Grace Breaks:** When you catch yourself being harsh or critical, pause and reframe with compassion.

The more you practice, the stronger these mental muscles get. Confidence doesn't appear overnight. It's built step by step, thought by thought. The same mind that creates fear also holds the power to calm it.

The same mind that creates fear also holds the power to calm it.

MENTAL HEALTH IS A SPECTRUM

One of the most powerful things I've learned from Chris Irwin is his perspective on physical and mental health.

There aren't just "fit" and "unfit" people or "healthy" and "unhealthy" ones—we're all on a spectrum, and we move up and down that spectrum based on the effort we put into taking care of ourselves. With physical health, that might be nutrition, movement, and rest. It's the same with mental health: You have to keep showing up for it daily.

Just like your body won't stay strong if you stop moving it, your mind won't stay well if you stop nurturing it.

When it comes to our minds, there aren't just people who "have issues" and people who don't. We're all on the same mental health continuum. Just as with physical fitness, we must put in daily effort to move toward the healthier end of the spectrum.

Of course, it's also important to acknowledge that some mental health conditions go beyond what we can manage on our own. Anxiety, depression, PTSD, OCD—these are real, complex challenges that often require professional support, treatment, or medication. Seeking help in those cases isn't a last resort; it's a powerful act of care and courage.

I love Chris's reminder that mental health isn't something you either have or don't have. It's something you work on. And the more you do, the stronger your mind becomes.

So instead of comparing yourself to someone who "has it all together," ask yourself, *What can I do today to support my own mental wellness?*

Maybe it's journaling or going for a walk. Maybe it's setting boundaries or saying no. Maybe it's finally booking that therapy appointment or simply remembering to take a breath and give yourself a little grace.

Whatever it looks like for you, mental fitness, just like physical fitness, isn't about perfection; it's about showing up and putting in the work. And every time you do, you move a little closer to the confident, grounded, real version of yourself you're meant to be.

LET'S TALK ABOUT MENTAL HEALTH

We never really know what someone else is going through ... which is exactly why we need to talk more openly about mental health.

It's especially important now, in a world that's constantly throwing challenges our way. We're all trying to keep up, all doing our best to hold it together, but underneath the surface, so many of us are quietly struggling.

For a long time, I didn't think of my fear as anything serious. I didn't even realize it was shaping my mental health. I just knew I didn't want anyone to see it. So, I kept it to myself and kept moving forward, hoping it would go away. It didn't.

It took me a long time to realize that mental health isn't something some people have and others don't. It's something we *all* have and something we all need to take care of. Fear, anxiety, self-doubt ... they're not just random emotions. They're signals. Clues that something inside needs attention.

One of the most powerful lessons I've learned is that mental health isn't black and white. You're not either "fine" or "not fine." We're all on a spectrum. Some days you feel strong. Other days, you're just getting through. And both are valid.

What matters is paying attention. Noticing where you are. And taking care of your mind the same way you'd care for your body. That's something I've become intentional about in my life—and with my kids too. I want them to know that taking care of their mental health is just as important as taking care of anything else.

For some of my kids, that means therapy. It gives them someone beyond our family to talk to—someone who listens, not to judge or "fix," but simply to understand. I'm so grateful that they're growing up in a world where that's becoming more normalized.

Rob and I do our best to be a safe place for our kids, but I also know that sometimes, you need more than just your parents. You need a full circle of people who've got your back. We've worked hard to build that for them, and watching them lean on it makes me hopeful, because I remember what it was like to not have that kind of support.

So many people still keep it all inside. They don't talk about what they're going through because they're afraid it will change how others see them. And they're not wrong; in fact, 58 percent of people with mental illness say worry about perception keeps them from seeking help.[59] But we need to change that. We need to be better at supporting one another—not only when life looks good, but when it doesn't.

And that starts with being okay with letting people in. Being okay with saying, "I'm struggling." Being okay with hearing someone else say the same. It's not always easy. But it matters more than we know. When we feel safe to be ourselves, and when we create that safety for the people we love, everything starts to shift.

WHAT FEARS ARE HOLDING YOU BACK?

If fear is keeping you from going after what you truly want, it's time to figure out what those fears are and start working through them. Ask yourself:

- What am I actually afraid of?
- What's holding me back?
- Am I afraid of being judged?
- Am I afraid of failing?
- Am I afraid of being alone?
- How could a different way of thinking help me move forward?

There are so many fears that try to stand between you and your dreams. But here's the thing—most of those fears aren't facts; rather, they're stories we tell ourselves. The longer we let those stories play on repeat, the more power they gain.

So, start questioning them.

While some fear can serve a purpose—keeping us safe, helping us stay alert—the rest is noise. That noise can get so loud that we forget what we're even reaching for.

That's why you have to do the work. Identify the fear. Reframe the thought. And start showing up for yourself anyway.

This is where your mental fitness comes in.

Whether it's Mirror Moments, gratitude journaling, affirmations, movement, or carving out time to care for your mind the way you care for your body—find what works for you and make it part of your daily rhythm.

Because when you build mental strength on purpose, fear doesn't get to run the show.

KEEPING IT REAL

TAKE ACTION IN SPITE OF FEAR

You don't have to eliminate fear before taking a step; you just have to take the step anyway. Let's do that now.

1. NAME THE FEAR.

Write down one fear that's been getting in your way lately. Don't overthink it. Just name it.

____

____

____

2. CHALLENGE THE STORY.

What are you telling yourself about this fear? ("I'll fail," "I'll look foolish," "It's too late.") Now, rewrite that story. What's a more honest, empowering version?

____

____

____

3. MAKE A CHOICE.

What's one thing you can do today—just one small thing—that moves you in the direction of what you want? Write it down. Commit to it.

____

____

____

4. TAKE THE STEP.

Don't wait until you feel ready. Take the step. Send the message. Apply for the opportunity. Say what needs to be said. Whatever it is—do it scared.

5. CHECK IN.

After you take that step, take a moment to check in with yourself. How did it feel? What did you learn? What fear lost its grip, even just a little?

____

____

____

Chapter Ten

YOU CAN'T POUR FROM AN EMPTY CUP

"Self-care is giving the world the best of you, not what's left of you."[60]

KATIE REED

In 2017, my dad was diagnosed with stage four lung cancer. His body was riddled with cancer before we even knew he was sick. He wasn't a smoker, so the diagnosis came as a complete shock.

It started with a cough. He'd always had allergies, so we assumed that was the cause. But when it lingered and wouldn't go away, he finally went in for a CT scan.

He called me after the results came in and said, "I just got a call from my doctor." I could tell by the sound of his voice that it wasn't good. He asked me to come with him and my mom to the doctor's office—he knew she'd have a hard time hearing what was coming.

That scan led to the diagnosis.

Later, a bone scan revealed that the cancer had already spread—his spine, his hips, almost everywhere.

What's wild is that he said he wasn't in pain. Maybe he had been living with it for so long that he didn't even realize something was wrong.

CANCER SUCKS

My dad fought hard. He tried every therapy available at the time—some so new they hadn't existed just a few years earlier. Watching him battle cancer was one of the hardest times of my life. I mean, how do you sit there and watch someone you love whittle away to almost nothing without falling apart yourself?

I went to every doctor's appointment and helped make decisions when needed. That part was especially hard for my mom. She had been the caretaker their entire marriage, but in those final months, the weight of it all was too much. After more than fifty years together, she just couldn't wrap her head around the idea of losing him, let alone making end-of-life decisions.

In the final month, my dad couldn't leave his room anymore. So, we brought his favorite recliner upstairs and set it up in the bedroom. That's where he spent most of his time—curled up in that chair, thin and tired.

The only thing he could stomach was Nutella on Challah bread. That was it. And some days he could barely manage to eat even that. He lost so much weight, he barely looked like himself anymore.

I moved into their home for that month, sleeping in their bedroom so I could be there at night if he needed anything. It gave my mom peace of mind, and honestly, it helped me too. Hospice nurses came, but I was still the one giving him his medications, managing his pain, and helping him with everything.

I remember him saying one day, "I just wish I could say goodbye and walk through a door. No suffering. Just peace."

But that's not how it happened. He suffered so much at the end. Everything hurt. His body was failing, and there was nothing I could do to stop it. That helplessness is something I'll never forget.

Cancer is brutal. Unfair. Relentless.

My dad didn't smoke. He lived a good life. He was active. He took care of himself. None of that mattered. Cancer still found its way in, a reminder that some things are beyond our control.

He fought for two full years. And on May 21, 2019, he took his last breath.

I only ever saw my dad cry three times in my life.

The first was when I came home with a black eye after my boyfriend hit me.

The second was when I left for college.

And the third was when he knew it was our last goodbye.

He will always be the man I compare everyone to. The first man I ever loved. The best father my sister and I could've asked for. He will always be my dad. And I will always miss him.

LIFE MUST KEEP MOVING

During the time my dad was sick, I didn't take care of myself. I didn't even think to ask what I needed. Every ounce of my energy—physical, emotional, mental—was poured into being there for him and my mom.

Before his diagnosis, my husband, my oldest son, and I had planned a big trip: hiking the Inca Trail in Peru. It was scheduled for June 2019, just a few weeks after my father's passing.

Now, if you've ever looked into the Inca Trail, you know it's no casual walk in the park. It's intense, high altitude, physically demanding, and definitely something you're supposed to train for.

Needless to say, I didn't train or prepare in any way. I couldn't, because in the months leading up to that trip, I was doing something far more important: I was being a daughter.

And then, in May, just weeks before the trip, my dad passed away.

We were faced with a decision: Do we still go, or do we stay?

It felt surreal. Everything was still so fresh. But deep down, I knew my dad wouldn't have wanted us to cancel. He was never one for sitting still. He would've said, "Go. Live your life."

So, we did.

For me, it wasn't just a trip. It was something I desperately needed. It was self-care in its rawest and most unexpected form. It was permission to breathe again.

There's so much guilt when someone you love dies. So many thoughts, so many emotions swirling around what you could've done and/or what you should be doing now. Taking that trip gave me the space I didn't even know I needed to start working through all of that.

Losing my dad was one of the saddest, hardest experiences of my life. I was there with him through it all—right up until the very end. And in the aftermath, I needed something that would shake me out of the fog. I needed something hard. Something different. Something that reminded me that life was still moving forward, and so was I.

Most of my friends supported the choice. But of course, not everyone did. I heard the whispers: "I can't believe she's going on a trip like that right after her dad passed away."

There's this unspoken expectation that grief is supposed to look a certain way—that you're supposed to wear it outwardly and visibly for a set amount of time before you're allowed to smile or breathe again.

But that's not how I see it. Grief doesn't follow a schedule. And it doesn't look the same for everyone. Grief has no schedule. Forward is still forward.

I recently spoke with a woman whose son died by suicide. Instead of locking herself away, she chose to celebrate life. It made people around her deeply uncomfortable, but she knew that was what *she* needed.

We all grieve in our own way. There's no "right" way to do it.

For me, the hike through Peru wasn't about checking something off a list. It was about coming back to myself. After months of heartache, of being so focused on someone else's needs, I needed something to wake me up again, to remind me that I was still strong. Still capable. Still moving forward.

It was the beginning of healing.

It was movement.

It was breath.

It was life.

And I think my dad would've been proud of that.

HIKING THE INCA TRAIL

The thing about doing something that puts you outside of your comfort zone is that it demands your full focus.

I was in terrible shape during that trip. I hadn't been to the gym in months, and the Inca Trail is not an easy hike. Yes, I had already climbed Mount Kilimanjaro, but this was different.

First of all, it was hot. Really hot. Sweat poured off me nonstop, and I longed for the days of writing my name in the Kilimanjaro snow with my Shewee.

Second, it's not a straight climb. You go up, then down, then back up again—all the way to over thirteen thousand feet. After spending months taking care of my dad, I wasn't physically or emotionally prepared for this kind of challenge.

Everything hurt. It was only a three-day hike, but after the first day, I honestly wanted to curl up on the side of the trail and sleep. I was just so exhausted.

But I didn't stop. I kept going. Even when I didn't think I could take another step, I did. I took the next one. And the next. I wanted to finish what I started.

The best thing about that trail was that it pulled me out of everything else. All I could really focus on was breathing and putting one foot in front of the other.

I wasn't thinking about what I could've done differently. I wasn't going over conversations or regrets. I wasn't even looking ahead. I was fully in the moment—step by step, breath by breath.

We saw people turn back because the trail was too hard. We saw others who were carried into camp after dark because they hadn't made it in time.

But I didn't turn around. I didn't get carried in. I kept moving forward. One painful, determined step at a time.

And with every single step, I felt my dad with me—cheering me on, reminding me that I could do hard things.

LET GO OF THE GUILT

The world may question the things we want, especially when it comes to taking care of ourselves.

Somehow, self-care still gets labeled as selfish. And because of that, every time we try to do something for ourselves, there's usually someone trying to make us feel guilty about it. And far too often, that someone … is us.

We've got to let go of the guilt and recognize self-care for what it really is: a vital act of self-love.

Love is almost always the guiding force in our care for others. Love should also be the driving force in caring for ourselves.

We need to practice self-care because it is the very thing that will give us the strength and capacity to continue to care for others. When we learn to ask ourselves what we want and prioritize our own self-care, we will be better parents, better children, better friends, and better humans.

As a parent, I want my kids to look at me and see that it's okay to take time for yourself. I want them to see that it makes me a better mother when I am rejuvenated rather than weary. I want them to understand that self-care will make them better rather than feel guilty for taking time away from their own future children or spouse.

Going back to the Inca Trail—when we finally made it to the Sun Gate, the first place on the trail where you can see Machu Picchu—it was just after sunrise. The sky had started to glow, the air was quiet, and that first glimpse of Machu Picchu below felt surreal. It was one of those moments where everything just stops, and you remember exactly where you are.

And in that moment, I felt my dad with me.

Not a trace of guilt. Just peace.

Even though some people's comments made me feel guilty for going, I knew in my heart that it was exactly what I needed. That trip gave me space to breathe again. To feel again. To start healing.

Letting go of the guilt doesn't mean ignoring our responsibilities; it means remembering that we matter too.

Sometimes, letting go of the guilt is as simple as reminding ourselves: If we're doing the best we can and showing up with love, then that's enough. Self-care is not selfish. It is how you keep showing up for the people you love.

Self-care is not selfish. It is how you keep showing up for the people you love.

MAKE SELF-CARE A PRIORITY

Somewhere along the way, many of us picked up this idea that self-care is indulgent. That it's optional. That it's something you get to do *after* everything else is handled. And when life gets full (which it always does), the first thing we cancel is our time for ourselves.

But the people who are relying on you need the version of you who's rested, grounded, and centered. The only way to be that version of you is to make yourself a priority.

I'm not talking about booking a five-day spa retreat—unless that's your thing, in which case, go for it. I'm talking about simple, consistent habits that support your well-being: a morning walk, a few deep breaths, a phone call with someone who makes you laugh, five minutes alone with your coffee before the rest of the house wakes up.

It doesn't have to be dramatic. It just has to be intentional.

Studies have shown that people who practice regular self-care experience real benefits: 64 percent report an increase in self-confidence. Another 64 percent say it helps them be more productive. And 71 percent say it makes them happier overall.[61]

Those aren't small numbers. That's not fluff. That's evidence that self-care matters.

So, here's what I'm going to invite you to do: Treat self-care like any other important commitment in your life. Put it on your calendar. Block the time. And whatever you do, don't cancel on yourself.

Because when you take care of yourself, everything else gets better. You're more patient. More focused. More present. You listen better. You respond instead of react. You bring calmer energy into the room, and the people around you feel that.

And here's the best part: When the people in your life see you making space for yourself without guilt, it gives them permission to do the same. You're not just taking care of yourself; you're modeling what healthy, sustainable living looks like.

Self-care is not a luxury. It's not selfish. It's a quiet, powerful way to say: *I matter too.* Put self-care on your calendar and do not cancel on yourself.

Put self-care on your calendar and do not cancel on yourself.

And you do. You always have.

SELF-CARE CAN BE SIMPLE

If you're not sure where to begin, start small. Ask yourself what you need right now—what feels good, what feels doable—and give yourself permission to do just that.

Self-care doesn't have to be elaborate or time-consuming. It can be as simple as five minutes with your journal, writing down one thing you're grateful for. It might be taking a short walk, stretching your body, or sitting in silence for a moment to just breathe.

You could try:

- Journaling to gather your thoughts or process your day.
- Meditation to clear your mind and create space for calm.
- A quick workout to relieve stress and get your energy moving.
- Aromatherapy, music, or candles to shift the atmosphere around you.
- Taking a short nap to recharge.
- Cooking, reading, or anything that feels creative or comforting.
- A therapy session to talk things through with someone supportive.

- A mental health day to reset and give yourself a break.

Whatever self-care looks like for *you*, honor that. Maybe it's big, maybe it's tiny. Either way, it matters.

Most of us are so busy taking care of others that we put ourselves at the very bottom of the list—if we make the list at all. But self-care isn't an indulgence. It's part of what helps us stay steady, connected, and whole.

SOME FINAL THOUGHTS

In the days after my dad's death, I was grateful I asked myself what I needed—and that I made the choice to hike the Inca Trail. Even though not everyone understood it, that trip gave me exactly what I needed at the time. It reminded me how vital self-care is, especially when life feels heavy and complicated.

As I put one foot in front of the other—tired, aching, and emotionally raw—I thought about all the moments my dad and I had shared. In the quiet of the trail, I found space to reflect, to breathe, and to begin moving forward.

That trip didn't erase the pain, but it gave me a way through it. It helped me reconnect with myself in a season when I had lost so much. With each step, I started rebuilding my confidence—not in a flashy or dramatic way, but in a quiet, steady one.

Confidence doesn't always come from the big wins. Sometimes it grows in the moments when we simply choose to take care of ourselves, even when everything else feels like it's falling apart.

Self-care will look different for each of us. But whatever it looks like for you, it matters. Ask yourself what you need. Make space for the things that fill you up. And then, give yourself permission to follow through.

Not because it's indulgent, but because it's necessary.

KEEPING IT REAL

A SELF-CARE RESET

Take a quiet moment—just you and your thoughts. This isn't about creating a perfectly balanced life. It's about checking in with what you need right now and giving yourself permission to show up for yourself.

1. Ask yourself: What do I need right now?
   Write down anything that comes to mind. Rest? Laughter? Movement? Connection? There's no wrong answer. Just be honest.

   ____

   ____

   ____

2. Think about something that brings you joy.
   It doesn't have to be big. A walk, a phone call, a song you love, a quiet cup of coffee. When was the last time you made time for it? When can you do it again?

3. Choose one small act of care.

   Pick something simple you can do for yourself in the next twenty-four hours. Write it down. Then do it. Not later. Not someday. Just soon.

   ____

4. Let go of the guilt.

   Write one sentence that releases you from the pressure to be everything to everyone: "Taking care of myself matters because ... " Say it out loud. Let yourself believe it.

   ____

   ____

   ____

5. Check your calendar.

   Where in the next week is there space for you? Block out a time—even if it's just fifteen minutes—and protect it like you would for anyone you love. Because you are someone you love too.

PILLAR #3 EXERCISES

ASK YOURSELF WHAT YOU WANT

If you want to learn how to truly know what you want, it's time to put your learning into practice. Here are ten different exercises to help build your confidence by asking yourself what you really want. Choose one of these exercises and follow through with it. You can come back and choose a different exercise as often as you need to. Remember—discovering what you want creates space for who you're meant to be. So don't skip these exercises. They are an important part to building REAL confidence.

1. DESIRE MAPPING

Write down ten things you want most in life right now. For each item, ask yourself:

- **Why do I want this?**
- **How would achieving this make me feel?**

Identify themes or emotions that stand out.

____

____

____

____

2. FUTURE-SELF LETTER

Write a letter from your future self, imagining you've achieved everything you want. Describe your life in detail:

- Where are you?
- What are you doing?
- How do you feel?

This helps clarify what you truly desire.

3. THE "WHAT IF" LIST

Write down ten things you'd do if failure weren't an option. Highlight the ones that feel most exciting or meaningful. Reflect on what they reveal about your wants and values.

4. JOY JOURNAL

For one week, write down moments that bring you joy or spark excitement. At the end of the week, review your journal to spot patterns. Use these insights to uncover what you truly want.

5. CLARITY THROUGH CONTRAST

Write a list of things you don't want in life. For each item, write the opposite—what you *do* want. For example:

- Don't want: "Feeling stuck in my job."
- Do want: "A career that challenges and inspires me."

____

____

____

____

____

____

6. THE "5 WHYS" EXERCISE

Identify something you think you want. Ask yourself "Why?" five times, digging deeper with each answer. This exercise helps uncover the core desire behind your want.

____

____

____

____

____

____

____

____

____

____

7. THE PASSION INVENTORY

Create three columns:

Activi- ties I enjoy.	Things I'm curious about.	Skills I want to develop.

Review your list to see what aligns with your true desires.

8. SILENT REFLECTION

Set aside ten minutes each day for quiet reflection. Ask yourself:

- "What do I truly want right now?"
- "What's stopping me from pursuing it?"
- Write down any thoughts or insights that arise.

9. VISION BOARD CREATION

Gather images, words, or symbols that represent what you want in life. Arrange them on a board and place it somewhere visible. Use it as a daily reminder of your goals and desires.

10. WEEKLY ALIGNMENT CHECK-IN

At the end of each week, ask yourself:

- "Did I take steps toward what I want this week?"
- "What can I do next week to move closer to my goals?"

Adjust your actions to stay aligned with your desires.

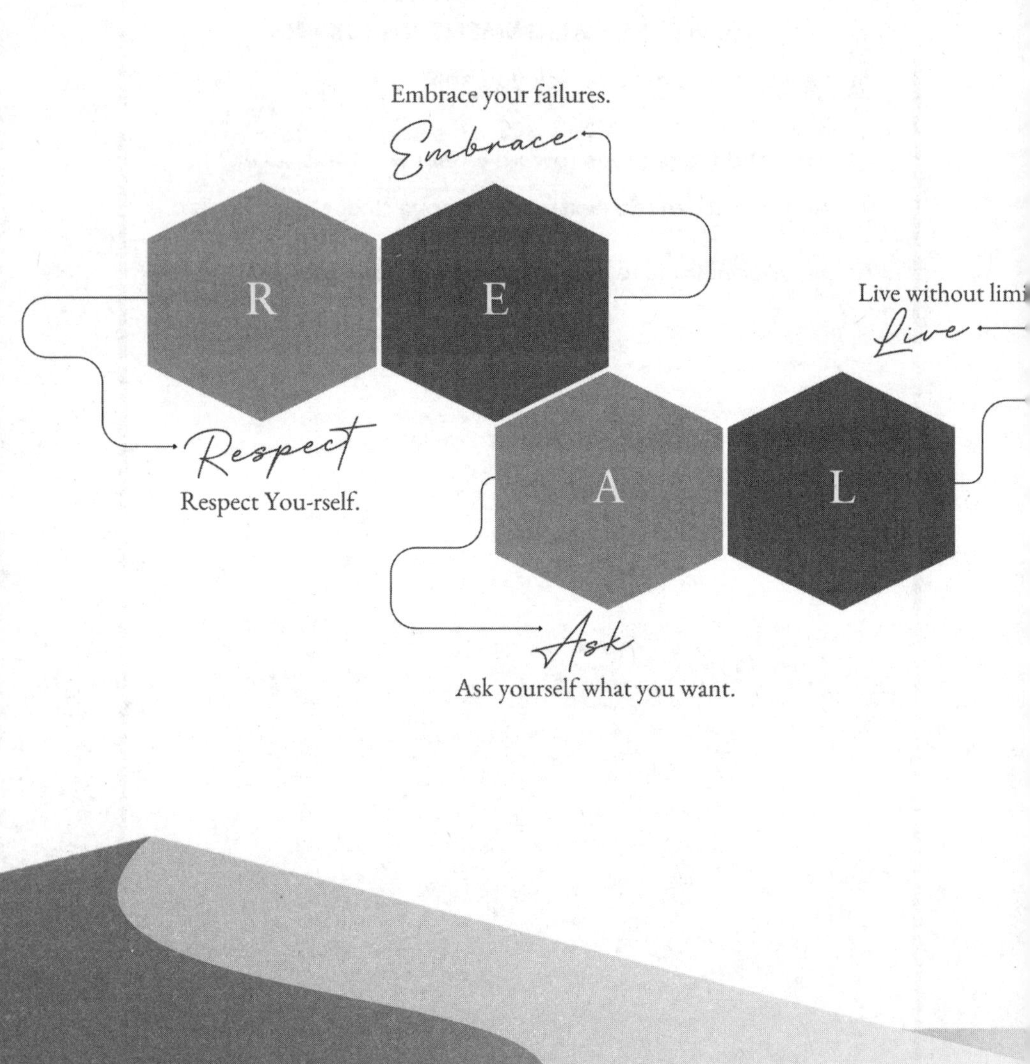
Embrace your failures.
Embrace
R
E
Live without limi
Live
Respect
Respect You-rself.
A
L
Ask
Ask yourself what you want.

PILLAR #4

LIVE WITHOUT LIMITS

Living without limits means breaking free from the boundaries we place on ourselves—even the ones we don't realize are there. It's about overcoming our doubts, focusing on our priorities, and owning our own story. It's embracing our true potential and living life in a way that feels authentic and bold.

At its heart, living without limits is about building REAL confidence. It's about knowing that you have what it takes to overcome whatever challenges may come. Every time you face a difficulty and push through, you build resilience. It becomes a cycle: The more you overcome, the more confident you become, and the fewer limits you see.

To live without limits means to let go of self-doubt, to challenge the status quo, and to take action every day toward a life that feels meaningful and free. It's about realizing that the only limits that exist are the ones we place on ourselves. By breaking free from those constraints, you can discover a world full of opportunities, growth, and endless possibilities.

Chapter Eleven

TURN DOWN THE VOLUME ON YOUR DAILY DOUBTS

"If you hear a voice within you say 'you cannot paint,' then by all means paint, and that voice will be silenced."[62]

VINCENT VAN GOGH

My mom grew up in a small, rural town in western Pennsylvania—the kind of place where everyone knew each other, and life was simple but hard. Her parents were immigrants—her mother from Hungary and her father from Czechoslovakia. Neither of them had much formal education. Her mom made it through sixth grade. Her dad worked long hours in the coal mines and later at the local brewery, bringing home just enough to keep the family going.

Most of what they ate, they grew. Most of what they had, they made. My mom learned how to do everything early. She could sew, can vegetables, cook a full meal, and tend animals before she was even in high school.

One of her jobs was collecting the eggs from the chickens each day, which sounds easy enough, until you learn that the chicken coop often had snakes hiding underneath the boards or coiled up in the nesting boxes. She said she'd bang on the side of the coop before going in, hoping the sound would scare them off, but sometimes they'd still be there, curled around the eggs. To this day, she hates snakes. I don't blame her.

There wasn't a lot of dreaming in her world. Girls were expected to cook, clean, and find someone to marry. That was the script. That was the life. No one asked her what she wanted to do or who she wanted to become. It was assumed she'd stay close to home and settle into the same pattern as everyone else.

But there was one thing her mother insisted on—good grades. My grandmother could be tough. If my mom came home with a 99, she'd hear, "Why not 100?" There wasn't much praise, just the expectation to do better, be better. It wasn't about opening doors to bigger opportunities; it was about discipline and respect. But those expectations, that push for perfection, gave my mom a kind of quiet determination that would end up changing everything.

When my mom was in the tenth grade, she walked into a library for the very first time. She still remembers that moment like it was yesterday. She had never seen anything like it. Shelves upon shelves of books—stories, knowledge, ideas—just sitting there waiting for her. For the first time in her life, she had the freedom to choose where she wanted to go, even if it was only in her imagination.

That library changed everything. It opened her world in ways she never knew were possible.

Around the same time, she moved into the home of a local physician and his wife to help care for their children. They were kind to her, and as she spent time with the family, she quietly observed the rhythm of their lives. She noticed the books on the shelves, the talk of school and work, the ease of a household where opportunities felt possible. She saw a life shaped by education, stability, and choice. For the first time, she could picture a future that didn't look like the one she had grown up around. And in those quiet moments, she let herself wonder: *What if that could be my life too?* That curiosity sparked something inside of her. Even though she still wrestled with daily doubts, those two experiences—the books and the exposure to a different kind of life—planted a dream she couldn't ignore.

She wanted more than what was expected of her—not because she looked down on the life she came from, but because she sensed she was capable of more than simply meeting everyone else's expectations. She wanted to learn, grow, and see what else the world had to offer.

So . . . she did.

She took the confidence she had, however small, and she used it to move forward. She poured her energy into school and focused on her education with everything she had. And, in 1957, at eighteen years old, she applied and was admitted to the University of Pittsburgh.

The library may have opened the door, but college changed the course of her entire life. Doubt gets quieter every time you act in spite of it.

Doubt gets quieter every time you act in spite of it.

BREAKING THE STEREOTYPES

Getting into college changed everything for my mom. It was her first real step outside the life she had always known, the beginning of a journey that would carry her beyond the poverty of her childhood, beyond the stereotypes she'd grown up with, and into a future she had once only dreamed about.

She didn't step into that future with REAL confidence. Not even close. She doubted herself constantly. She had daily worries about whether she was smart enough, whether she belonged, whether she'd be able to keep up. But she kept going anyway.

While she was in college, she worked three jobs to cover tuition and living expenses. She lived frugally, studied late, and kept pushing forward because she had a vision of something different for her life, something bigger.

In 1961, she was accepted into medical school at the University of Pittsburgh. It was a bold move in a time when very few women pursued medicine. Out of one hundred and twenty students in her class, only five were women. But all five of them graduated and went on to practice.

And my mom? She practiced medicine for decades, continuing well into her late sixties.

But here's the part I love most: If you asked her whether she loved her career, she'd say yes. And if you asked her whether she loved cooking and cleaning and caring for her family, she'd also say yes.

Neither answer was based on a sense of obligation, but because she had made the choice. She chose to be a doctor, and she chose to be a wife and mother. Those choices gave her power—the power to be content with the life she had made for herself.

She redefined what it meant to be a woman in her generation. She didn't reject tradition, but she didn't let it define her either. She wove together the parts of her life that mattered most to her and made something completely her own.

And even though she never felt completely confident, she showed up anyway. She did the hard things—not because she had no doubts, but because she didn't let those doubts have the final say.

WE ALL HAVE DAILY DOUBTS

No matter who you are, you will face irritating, frightening, and/or intimidating seasons of doubt. How do I know? Because we all do. It's inescapable. Even the boldest, most confident among us has to deal with a nagging sense of doubt every now and then.

You might wake up stressed about the day ahead. Maybe you question whether you really deserved that raise, or whether you're qualified enough to apply for the job you want. Maybe you wonder if you said the wrong thing in a meeting—or if people are judging you for ordering the fried chicken instead of the salad when you're out with friends.

Daily doubts show up everywhere. They're the negative thoughts that sneak in when you're making decisions, or the voice in your head that replays unkind or insincere comments. They chip away at your confidence. They tell you you're not good enough, not ready enough, or not worthy enough—and they keep you from living fully or going after what you really want.

The more we listen to those doubts, the louder they get. Before long, we're stuck in our own heads, circling endlessly, consumed by the What-if Whisperer.

Everyone has their own version of this. We all have things that make us question ourselves or second-guess our decisions. Those doubts might seem small or unimportant, but even the little ones can be enough to hold you back.

If my mom had listened to the doubts—her own, or the ones other people tried to place on her—she never would've become a doctor.

She wasn't handed that dream. She created it.

She moved forward even when she wasn't sure. She believed in what was possible, even when others didn't.

And that's what made the difference.

Because when you stop letting doubt steer the ship, when you trust yourself enough to move forward anyway, you open the door to a life that's bigger than fear. You start living without limits.

Confidence isn't the absence of doubt—it's choosing to move forward anyway.

Confidence isn't the absence of doubt–it's choosing to move forward anyway.

BEING A WOMAN IN A MAN'S WORLD

If you're one of only five women in a class where men constantly remind you that your voice doesn't matter, it takes a toll.

My mom was a woman working in a male-dominated field, and while she was strong and determined, it's no surprise that she struggled with confidence at times. The messages she received, both spoken and unspoken, kept telling her she didn't belong.

She earned less than her male colleagues for many years. Unfortunately, that hasn't changed much. Even today, female doctors earn significantly less than their male counterparts—by as much as two million dollars over a forty-year career.[63] Hiring discrimination, gender bias, and lack of salary transparency all contribute to that gap. And it's not just in medicine. It's across industries.[64] My mother had every reason to feel limited by the world around her. But she didn't let it stop her.

She worked hard, and even though it took effort to hold it all together, she kept going.

I remember she was always reading the latest self-help books on communication, confidence, and mindset. She was constantly looking for ways to grow and be better. I'm sure she wrestled with impostor syndrome more than once, even though she was one of the best at what she did.

And eventually, people saw it too—her quiet brilliance, her drive, her way of making others feel seen. What she had been working so hard to build on the inside finally started to show on the outside.

She became a leader in her field. She went into what was called "chest and breast imaging," specializing in mammograms, chest X-rays, and needle biopsies. She published hundreds of papers. She loved her work because it helped people, and that's what made her great.

My mom didn't shatter the glass ceiling by pretending doubt didn't exist. She shattered it by walking forward anyway.

She didn't let a system designed to minimize her voice shake her confidence. She kept showing up and doing what she was meant to do.

And because of that, she didn't just live a good life—she lived a meaningful one. A bold one. A life without limits.

REMEMBER WHAT YOU WERE MADE FOR

One of the things I love most about my mom is that she never gave in to her doubts—at least not for long. She was a doer. She didn't wait around for permission. Instead, she looked for ways to move forward, even when the world told her she couldn't.

When she was struggling, she had this little poem she would say to herself. I don't know who wrote it or where it came from, but it stuck with her:

What did you make me for, dear God?
Why did you waste your time on me?
You could have made a tree to shade the tired.
Or a flower to catch one's breath.
Why did you waste your time on me?
You spent your time on me because I can change the world.

She recited it like a quiet mantra, especially on the hard days. It was her way of reminding herself of her purpose, of her ability to do meaningful things, even when doubt tried to convince her otherwise.

What I learned from watching her wasn't just about ambition or achievement. It was about identity. It was about believing that you are here for a reason, even when other people can't see it. *Especially* then.

Because when you believe you were made for something more, the way you see yourself changes. And when you change the way you see yourself, the world around you starts to shift too.

That's what my mom taught me:

You don't have to silence every doubt.

You just have to trust that you were made for more. And you have to keep going anyway.

DON'T LET THEIR DOUBTS DEFINE YOUR DECISIONS

One of the things I've experienced again and again is people questioning my choices. More often than not, it's less about me and more about them—*their* fears, *their* insecurities, *their* belief in limitations they've never questioned.

When we decided to adopt, the people closest to us celebrated. They knew our hearts. But others? They had questions. Not in a cruel way, but in casual conversations, almost as if they couldn't quite understand.

"Are you sure you can handle that?"

"Do you really know what you're getting into?"

"Why would you adopt when you can have more biological kids?"

Those questions were heavy, even if they weren't meant that way. And my answer was simple: there are so many amazing kids in the world waiting for a family to love them, and we wanted to be that family.

That's the thing. When you're going after something big, not everyone will understand it, and not everyone will support you. But you can't let their doubts become your truth. You have to know where your confidence comes from so that every yes is rooted in your own wants, desires, and authenticity. You have to be able to separate your own thoughts from the noise of other people's opinions. And above all, you have to believe that you are capable of growing into whatever your yes requires of you.

When we adopted, I didn't need everyone else to agree. I needed to stay rooted in why we said yes. And we did. Because we believed we could.

Belief is powerful.

Confidence comes from choosing to move forward, step by step, regardless of who questions you along the way.

YOUR THOUGHTS ARE NOT REALITY

If you're anything like me, daily doubts have a way of sneaking into your mind, chipping away at your confidence when you least expect it.

Maybe you've heard thoughts like these:

- Nobody's interested in my ideas.
- I've made too many mistakes.
- Now's not the right time.
- It's too risky.
- I'm not smart enough.
- I'm not thin enough.

These thoughts show up uninvited, often at the worst possible moments. And while they might *sound* like truth, they're not. They're just thoughts. But when we start to believe them, they can easily become limiting beliefs that hold us back.

We retreat. We play small. We stay stuck.

But here's the truth: Your thoughts are not reality.

You can't control every thought that pops into your head, but you *can* choose which ones you listen to.

I've told my kids for years, "You can do anything you put your mind to." And I've seen them prove it over and over again. But to truly build REAL confidence, you have to learn to separate fact from fiction. You have to stop letting your doubts write your story.

Because if you believe the lie that you're not good enough, or ready enough, or worthy enough ... that becomes your reality.

However, when you challenge those thoughts and replace the lies with truth, you create a different reality. One where you're capable. One where you *move forward anyway.*

The next time your thoughts start swirling, remember this: **they're just thoughts.** You don't have to believe them. You don't have to follow them. And you certainly don't have to let them steal your confidence. You can't always control your thoughts, but you can choose which ones to believe.

You can't always control your thoughts, but you can choose which ones to believe.

The biggest battle you'll ever fight is the one that happens in your own mind.

So, choose your thoughts with care. Feed your mind with truth. And when doubt whispers that you can't ... show up anyway.

Because *that's* how confidence grows. And that's how you start living without limits.

FIVE WAYS TO BUILD CONFIDENCE IN ADVERSITY

Everyone faces challenges. It's one of the few things we all have in common. If you're going through something hard right now, I want you to know—you're not alone.

And once you truly believe that, it becomes a little easier to loosen the grip of those daily doubts that whisper, *You're the only one struggling.* You're not.

Confidence doesn't come from a perfect life; it's built in the mess. In the difficulty. In showing up anyway. Here are five ways to start building REAL confidence—even when life feels anything but easy.

1. See the Good in Your Circumstances

When hard things happen (and they will), look for the good. That doesn't mean ignoring your pain or pretending everything's okay; instead, look for the moments that grow you, provide clarity, sharpen your resilience, and shift your perspective.

Every challenge holds a lesson if we're willing to look for it. Choosing to look for it shifts your mindset—and that shift builds confidence.

2. Build Resilience and Perseverance

We grow through our trials, and the setbacks we usually kick ourselves for aren't signs that we're not capable but rather invitations to keep going, to get creative, and to build something stronger.

When you experience a setback, pick yourself back up and keep going. You're not starting over; you're starting wiser.

3. Shift from Fear to Opportunity

Fear is sneaky. It convinces us to shrink, to wait, to stop before we even begin. But what if we saw fear as a signal—not that something's wrong, but that something really matters? You unlock your ability to grow the moment you start seeing fear as an opportunity instead of a stop sign.

4. Practice Self-Compassion and Forgiveness

We are so hard on ourselves. We beat ourselves up for not being stronger, faster, or better. But confidence doesn't come from perfection; it comes from grace. You are not your setbacks. You are not your worst day.

When you can treat yourself with the same kindness you offer others, you build the kind of confidence that lasts—the kind that helps you keep going, no matter what.

5. Lean on Others and Learn from Their Stories

You don't have to do this alone.

There are people out there who've walked through the fire and made it to the other side. Let them walk with you. Let their stories remind you that healing is possible and confidence is rebuildable. Support is wisdom, not weakness.

YOUR MINDSET DETERMINES YOUR DESTINY

You might think your destiny is written in the stars, but the truth is, how you see the world determines how you move through it.

Overcoming daily doubts and living without limits starts with your mindset. You have to get really honest about the stories you're telling yourself—and whether they're even true.

Take a step back and look at whatever you're struggling with right now. Are you responding to reality, or are you reacting to old fears, insecurities, or assumptions that don't hold up anymore?

Most of my daily doubts in the past came down to feeling unworthy. I skipped events because I didn't think I'd fit in. I told myself I didn't dress the right way, wasn't the right age, or just didn't belong.

So many of those thoughts held me back from fully living my life. But I don't live in that space anymore. And I don't want you to either.

So let me say it clearly: Whatever doubts you're having about yourself—let them go. They are not the truth. You are stronger, smarter, and more capable than you give yourself credit for.

I don't let those daily doubts drive my life anymore. I know that nothing from my past gets to decide who I am now or where I go next.

The things I used to believe about myself, those self-imposed limits and made-up stories, I see them for what they are now. And I've let them go.

These days, I ask myself what I want—and I go after it. Fully. Confidently. Authentically.

That's what I want for you too.

You are enough. Exactly as you are. So let go of those doubts. Give yourself permission to stop holding back and start really living.

Because your confidence is already inside you. Once you believe that, you really can live a life without limits.

KEEPING IT REAL

A MINDSET SHIFT

Choose one daily doubt you've been carrying—just one. Maybe it's something you've believed about yourself for years, or maybe it's a thought that's been quietly showing up lately. Write it down.

____

____

Now, gently challenge that thought.

- Where did this belief come from?
- Is it actually true—or just something you've rehearsed so many times that it feels true?
- What would your day look like if you didn't believe that thought anymore?

Then, write a new belief to replace it. Something that feels empowering, honest, and true to who you are.

____

____

EXAMPLE:

Old thought: *"I'm not qualified enough to lead."*

New belief: *"I'm learning, growing, and showing up—and that makes me a powerful leader."*

Chapter Twelve

FOCUS ON WHAT MATTERS MOST

"Decide what kind of life you actually want, then say no to everything that isn't that."[65]

BRIANNA WIEST

Being a woman today is like navigating an endless maze of contradictions.

The pressure to avoid mistakes and failure is a never-ending battle. And rarely do we get recognition for our efforts.

Society piles on the pressure to be flawless and is all too happy to point out our imperfections.

We're told we can conquer anything, do anything, and be anyone we want to be. But if we assert ourselves a tad too much, we're labeled aggressive.

Take motherhood. It's glorified in theory, but heaven forbid we actually talk about our kids.

Career success? Oh, it's essential. But we must still be the nurturing, empathetic souls that society demands.

And in the end, our career should never get in the way of society's expectations of what a mother is supposed to do and be. We just have to figure out how to perfectly do both.

In everything we do, we're expected to strike a balance—assertive but not aggressive, compassionate but not too soft.

In the workforce, we have to lead with unwavering strength while avoiding the dreaded "overbearing" label. And we must support others, but not at the expense of our own ambitions.

When women call out injustices, we're known as troublemakers. Men doing the same? They're problem-solvers. If we're assertive, we're bossy. Men, however, are seen as natural-born leaders.

And what about our bodies? That is another battlefield all on its own.

Fitness is a tightrope walk. We're told to take care of our bodies but not to be "too obsessed." To stay in shape, but not too thin. To love ourselves as we are—but also to lose those last ten pounds. The message is confusing, but underneath it all, it's clear: Your weight matters. Not just your health, but also your appearance. And that pressure doesn't just live at the gym. It follows you everywhere.

Beauty standards are also a paradox. Beauty is the standard. But we should never be so beautiful that it threatens other women or causes bad behavior in men. We are told to age gracefully but never show signs of aging.

As a rule, we should never be rude, boastful, or selfish. Showing fear or vulnerability is not an option.

We're supposed to stand out while fitting in.

We're supposed to support other women in an environment that champions competition.

And above all, we're supposed to be grateful despite the complete and utter unfairness of it all.

I don't know about you, but the pressure to be perfect, to never falter, to always be pleasant, and to juggle conflicting demands is exhausting to me.

Despite our best efforts, it often feels like we're doing everything wrong and that the blame rests squarely on our shoulders. Watching every woman twist herself into knots to be liked and accepted is so hard to watch. That's why something has got to give. We have to start seeing ourselves and the world differently, or we'll keep living by everyone else's rules instead of our own.

THERE'S NO SUCH THING AS BALANCE

With so many expectations surrounding what we're supposed to do and be as women, life can get pretty complicated. We're constantly bombarded with messages about who we should be and how we should live. As women, not only do we feel that we have to do it all, but we have to do it all *well.*

This kind of thinking can lead to an overwhelming feeling of failure and a complete lack of confidence. We are literally setting ourselves up to fall when we follow this line of thinking.

We seek balance because we think balance is the key to doing it all.

But guess what? I'm not a believer in balance.

Balance doesn't exist.

I believe we have to prioritize what we're doing while we're doing it.

Sometimes your family will come first. Other times, your work will take precedence. And sometimes, your focus might need to be on your community. But wherever you choose to invest your time and energy, just know this: There is no way to balance it all equally, all the time. It's impossible to juggle all the balls at once.

When I'm on stage, I'm obviously not available to take a call from my child. Most of the time, I don't even have my phone on me. In those moments, my focus is completely on my audience. Although I will always be a devoted mother, I can't be available at every single moment, because in that moment, my attention is needed somewhere else.

On the flip side, when one of my kids is in crisis, I'm not putting work first. I'm putting them first. When I'm with them, I try to be fully with them. That's where my energy goes.

You can't expect yourself to do everything, let alone do it perfectly. Perfection doesn't exist, and there has to be some give and take.

Living without limits doesn't mean doing everything at once. It means being intentional. It's about managing the moments and making each one count.

When you're parenting, focus on being the best parent you can be. When you're working, give your work your full energy. Trust that you're where you need to be. And don't waste time feeling guilty about the rest.

The more you release the pressure to balance it all, the more confidence you'll feel in each moment. Life feels more manageable when you stop trying to do it all and instead show up fully where you are. Because life isn't about doing everything. It's about being present in the moments that matter most. Balance isn't the goal. Presence is.

Balance isn't the goal. Presence is.

THE MOMENTS YOU GIVE YOURSELF MATTER MOST

Let me say it again: I don't believe in balance. Not the way it's often sold to women. You can't give 100 percent to everything all the time. That math doesn't work. The problem is, we spend so much time trying to "balance it all" that we forget we're part of the equation. We forget to check in on the one person holding all the pieces together.

We wake up, pack lunches, head to work, sit in meetings, answer emails, check off errands, make dinner, fold laundry, and somewhere in there, maybe eat a granola bar and call it lunch. And we call that balance? Let's be real. It's not about balance. It's about priorities. And sometimes, that priority needs to be you.

Taking care of yourself mentally, physically, and emotionally isn't selfish. It's essential. You can't give what you don't have.

So, take the walk. Take the nap. Take the time.

Whatever *your thing* is, do it, and don't apologize for it.

When you give yourself those moments, you show up better for everything and everyone else that matters in your life. That's not balance. That's wisdom.

LEARN WHAT WORKS FOR YOU

Maybe you're someone who believes in balance. You may believe that you can create balance by spending a certain amount of time with family, a certain amount of time at work, and maybe even some time for just yourself scheduled in there.

Some people may be exceptionally good at balancing their time to accomplish all their tasks and attend to every person who's clamoring for a piece of them. But it doesn't work for me.

I used to beat myself up constantly because I simply couldn't do it all. That went on for years ... until I learned to give myself grace. The truth is, things won't always work out the way you schedule them. And sometimes, things aren't going to go the way you think they're going to go.

When those things happen, rather than letting it chip away at your confidence, show yourself grace and give yourself permission to pivot. That's what living life without limits is all about: the ability to not be locked into just one way of doing things, even if that means doing things outside of the norm.

It's okay to order out for dinner when the day has run away from you. There were so many school nights when the best I could do was take the kids through a drive-through or order takeout. It's okay to carpool so that you don't have to be at every rehearsal. I've missed plenty of rehearsals and games in my life.

My daughter Mili graduated from eighth grade the same night my husband and I had to leave for a trip we'd planned for our birthdays. It wasn't intentional. We were supposed to leave the next day, but a weather system was coming in, and our flight got canceled. If we wanted to make it to South Africa, we had to leave a day early. And that meant missing her graduation.

Did I feel guilty? Of course I did.

But she understood. Her siblings were there to cheer her on, and she knew we were thinking about her the whole time.

We can't be so hard on ourselves that we forget we're human. Sometimes, we have to make choices that don't look picture-perfect on the outside, but they're the right choices for where we are in that moment.

What works for one person is not necessarily going to work for someone else. You have to figure out what works best for you and stop feeling guilty about it. Throw out the idea that you have to get it right every time. Life's messy. You're allowed to adjust.

We're all just doing the best we can with the life we've been given—and that's more than enough. Grace is the bridge between where you are and where you want to be.

Grace is the bridge between where you are and where you want to be.

RECOGNIZE EVERYONE'S LIFE IS DIFFERENT

When we're doing our best to manage all the things life throws at us, I think it's important to remember that everyone's life experience is different.

It's not fair or helpful to look at another woman and judge her for what she is (or isn't) doing. We don't know her circumstances. Some women are juggling demanding careers while raising children. Others are caring for aging parents, managing health challenges, or rebuilding after a major life transition. We all have different capacities and different seasons.

I've seen firsthand how hard it is to navigate both professional ambition and motherhood. And when I think about that challenge, I often think of my friend Sarah.

Sarah is a partner in a large accounting firm. She's spent decades navigating the pressures of a male-dominated industry while raising her children and trying to stay grounded in what matters most.

When she started her career in the mid-1990s, the expectations were clear—and narrow. Women wore skirts or dresses and pantyhose. That was just how it was. Pants weren't really considered professional for women, and there were all these unspoken rules about how you had to look and act to be taken seriously.

Meanwhile, her male colleagues faced far fewer expectations. No one commented on what they wore or how they spoke. Sarah, like many women, felt the pressure to show up flawlessly—both in appearance and performance.

Even as the dress codes relaxed and times changed, Sarah continued to face subtle (and sometimes not-so-subtle) challenges. There were moments when clients, often male executives, seemed more at ease working with her male colleagues. While she didn't let it stop her, those moments served as a clear reminder of the double standards women still face.

Sarah's story is a reminder that what *looks* like confidence and composure on the outside often comes from years of pushing through invisible barriers.

It's also a reminder that we need to give each other more grace.

We never know what someone else is carrying. We never know what they're pushing through just to be there. So instead of judging or comparing, let's acknowledge that we're all doing the best we can with the lives we have and in the season we're in.

PRIORITIZING FAMILY AND WORK

When Sarah became a mother, the balancing act grew even more precarious. She felt she couldn't say no to career demands, especially knowing that many of her male colleagues didn't carry the same responsibilities at home.

Now, to be clear, Sarah's husband was a great partner. He helped a lot with the kids and supported her every step of the way. But even with that support, Sarah carried the invisible load so many women do: the mental to-do lists, the emotional weight, the constant recalibrating between work and home.

While most of the men she worked with had spouses managing the household and kids full-time, Sarah was navigating both worlds—coordinating the schedules, remembering the birthdays, leading teams, showing up at work events, and still making it to hockey games and golf tournaments.

She often thought about the moments she missed and felt the sting of them. So she pushed herself harder at home to make up for it. That constant drive to overcompensate, to excel both at work and as a parent, is something many working moms know all too well.

Despite her best efforts, Sarah still faced judgment. When she didn't attend social events or volunteer opportunities, some people assumed she was cold or detached. When she brought her laptop to her son's hockey practice, it wasn't because she didn't care about connecting with others; it was because working then allowed her to be fully present with her kids later.

What might look like disinterest from the outside is often a carefully calculated decision to protect what matters most. Sarah chose staying home and reading to her kids over grabbing drinks after work. Others may have thought she was being unfriendly, but she knew her time was precious, and she had learned how to prioritize what she had.

That's exactly what Michael Hyatt has spent years teaching. Hyatt, a bestselling author and leadership mentor, built his career helping high achievers focus on what really matters. In his book *Free to Focus*, he emphasizes that every yes carries an implicit no. Time management, as Hyatt defines it, isn't about squeezing more onto our plates. It's about being intentional with tradeoffs so that our yeses and noes align with the kind of life we want to live.[66]

GRACE OVER JUDGMENT

One of the most powerful lessons we can take from Sarah's story is the importance of both giving and receiving grace. We're all doing the best we can. Whether a woman works outside the home, stays home full-time, or does something in between—there is no single "right" way to do life.

What matters most is that we lift one another up rather than tear each other down.

When we support each other, we strengthen each other's confidence. Every path is valid. Every choice is personal. And every woman deserves to feel seen in the life she's creating.

Sarah's children—kind, compassionate, and well-rounded—are a testament to the life she poured herself into. What kept her grounded was knowing she was doing her best for her family, even though she wasn't doing it all perfectly. That was enough. That's all any of us can really do.

Her journey reminds us that confidence is about owning your priorities, showing yourself grace when life pulls you in different directions, and extending that same grace to others.

In a world full of expectations, Sarah's story challenges us to remember that we are already enough. And sometimes, living without limits simply means letting go of the limits we've placed on ourselves, or accepted from others, without even realizing it.

STOP LIVING THE PERFECT LIE

As women, we sometimes fall into the "perfect" trap. As I've mentioned before, when I was a stay-at-home mom, I felt like everything had to be perfect. With my first child, everything had to be sterilized, the house had to be completely clean all the time, and the meals had to be ready the instant my husband came in from work every evening.

I felt like I had to be June Cleaver, the stereotypical 1950s housewife from the old *Leave It to Beaver* TV show: the perfect wife, the perfect mother, and the perfect homemaker.

I had friends at the time who took it even further than that. They would not only ensure the house was clean and dinner was on the table, but they would also ensure that they were dressed up (lipstick and all) when their husbands came home. That way, they looked more *desirable*.

I'm hearing more about this mindset making a comeback for both men and women. People call it the "trad wife," or "traditional wife." If it really is coming back, it feels like stepping backward in time. Recent surveys show that the number of women who say they favor a return to traditional gender roles is growing, rising from about 23 percent in 2022 to 37 percent in 2024.[67] This isn't happening in a vacuum. Social media trends, cultural nostalgia, and the constant pressure to "do it all" are pushing some women to believe that stepping back into old roles is the only way forward.

Here's the truth: There's nothing wrong with choosing a traditional role—*if it's truly your choice.* The danger isn't in staying home, building a family, or wanting a slower pace. The danger is when that decision comes from pressure, comparison, or a belief that one version of womanhood is better than another.

I certainly felt that pressure for perfection, but it wasn't called being a "trad wife" then—it was simply the societal expectation. But the message was the same: be everything to everyone, make it look effortless, and don't admit when you're struggling.

Different pressures, same result. We end up chasing an impossible standard. We compare ourselves to a fictitious woman who doesn't even exist. We feel like we need to achieve something completely unattainable. And we let that illusion of perfection chip away at our confidence.

We've got to stop pretending that perfection is possible, because it's not. We will never be the perfect wife, mother, daughter, or friend. But we can certainly be a good one.

When our second child came along, things changed a bit, as they often do. There was no time to sterilize everything. Dinners became simpler. And I definitely wasn't dressing up. I was trying my best to get through the day.

Of course, as I watched other women who seemed to be able to do it all, there was still a sense that I was doing it wrong. But slowly, I let go of the illusion, which ironically allowed me to be a better mother and wife.

When your focus is no longer perfection, you can spend your time and energy on the things that really matter. You'll find that letting go of the unrealistic expectations increases your confidence and overall happiness. You free up space for the really important things. You stop wasting energy on appearances and start showing up for your life in a way that feels real and grounded.

Letting go of the "be perfect" lie won't just ease the pressure; it'll give you the freedom to live with more joy, more confidence, and a whole lot more grace.

IT'S OKAY TO BE OFF-BALANCE

The older I get, the more I realize that we are all just doing our best. And honestly? Our best is enough.

People love to toss around the mantra, "Fake it till you make it." I can't stand that way of thinking. I don't believe in faking anything. If you're struggling, let someone know. If life feels overwhelming, say it out loud. You don't need to put on a performance.

Confidence comes from speaking truth, even when it's hard. It comes from showing up with honesty and reminding yourself of who you are—over and over—until you believe it.

Nobody's life is perfect. We all have those messy, chaotic seasons that drive us crazy, and pretending things are fine when they're not doesn't help anyone. It just isolates us even further.

Rather than hiding behind the idea of *perfection*, why not open the door and invite *connection* instead?

Yes, there will be toys on the floor. There will be laundry on the couch and dishes in the sink. Every family home has a little bit of chaos. That's not failure. That's life.

But somewhere along the way, we started telling ourselves that the "perfect mother" has a spotless home, gourmet meals, and matching outfits for every kid, and we started holding ourselves to that ridiculous standard.

We have to stop. Because perfection is a made-up fantasy that does nothing but chip away at our confidence.

That was crystal clear to me by the time we got to kid number three, when we officially became outnumbered. And kids four through six? Any illusion of having control went out the window. We were playing a full-on zone defense and hoping for the best.

Some mornings, I thought I had it all together … until we'd pull up to school and one of the kids would casually say, "Um … Why doesn't Noah have any shoes on?" And there it was. The moment that reminded me: Life doesn't care how on top of things you felt five minutes ago.

After that, I learned to keep an extra pair of shoes in the car—because life happens. And you adjust.

Life isn't perfectly balanced. And that's okay. Some days, your patience is short, the oatmeal is cold, and the laundry pile is taller than your toddler. But those days are real. And *real* matters more than *perfect.* Besides, the idea of *perfect* is exhausting … and at least *real* lets you wear sweatpants.

So don't let the mess steal your joy. Don't let the chaos convince you you're doing it wrong. And never let anyone make you feel small for how your journey looks.

You're not here to be perfect. You're here to live fully, love deeply, and do your best with the life in front of you.

That's more than enough.

LIFE IS ABOUT PRIORITIES, NOT BALANCE

You can't live without limits if you're constantly pulled in a hundred directions, trying to give everything your all. That's why we need to talk about something that's just as essential to confidence as self-talk or mindset shifts:

We need to talk about priorities.

Some of the best advice I've ever received is that everything is *important,* but not everything is *urgent.* That's why we need to prioritize. We can't do everything at once or get it all done in a day. That's what tomorrow is for.

That's why I make a list of daily priorities every single morning—always on a pink piece of paper. Why pink? Because I'll lose it otherwise. A plain white sheet gets swallowed by the chaos of kids, counters, and clutter. But a pink one? That stands out.

That pink piece of paper has become my personal confidence boost. Each time I cross something off, I feel accomplished. Capable. On track.

Confidence grows when you can see the evidence of your effort. That's why REAL confidence doesn't come from achieving balance but from knowing what matters *right now* and giving *that thing* your full focus.

Whether you're raising kids, building a career, doing both, or finding your own path entirely, chances are, you're searching for some kind of balance.

If that's you, I want to gently invite you to let that go.

Instead of chasing balance, try identifying your true priorities. Learn to separate what's urgent from what's simply important. Design your day around what really needs your energy.

And then? Watch your confidence grow with every little win. You may realize it wasn't balance you were craving at all, but rather peace, clarity, and a bit more ease.

I believe many of us chase balance thinking it'll bring joy or contentment. But often, the pursuit of balance just leads to more pressure. More guilt. More stress.

While you're busy trying to "balance it all," you miss the beautiful, messy, meaningful moments right in front of you.

So instead of striving for balance, ask yourself: What matters most right now?

What does your work need from you when you're there? What does your family need when you're with them? And what do you need when you're finally alone?

Life is about being present in the moment you're in—and making that moment count. It's about focusing on what's urgent and giving yourself permission to let the rest wait.

Because when you stop chasing balance and start prioritizing what matters, your confidence will grow, and you'll start living life without limits. You don't need perfect balance. You need clear priorities and the courage to honor them.

You don't need perfect balance. You need clear priorities and the courage to honor them.

KEEPING IT REAL

REALITY CHECK-IN

Before you turn the page, take a moment for yourself. Grab a pen, a bright piece of paper (yes, the one you won't lose), and answer these three simple questions:

1. WHAT ACTUALLY MATTERS TODAY?

Not everything. Just the top three things that truly need your energy right now. List them.

____

____

____

2. WHERE DO YOU FEEL STUCK—OR STRETCHED?

Be honest with yourself. Are you telling yourself "I can't"? Or are you starting to notice your growth? Name where you are and give yourself credit for being real about it.

____

____

____

3. WHAT'S ONE THING YOU CAN DO TODAY THAT SUPPORTS YOUR CONFIDENCE?

It doesn't have to be big. Maybe it's asking for help. Saying no. Going for a walk. Speaking up in a meeting. Choose one thing that moves you forward.

____

____

____

This is your reminder that progress is personal. You don't need to prove anything to anyone. You just need to keep showing up—for yourself.

Chapter Thirteen

OWN YOUR STORY

"You either walk into your story and own your truth, or you live outside of your story, hustling for your worthiness."[68]

BRENÉ BROWN

Public speaking was never really my thing.

I didn't like standing up in front of a group. It always felt awkward and unnatural, like I was performing a version of myself I didn't quite believe in. So, in college, I signed up for a public speaking course, thinking maybe if I faced the fear head-on, it would magically go away.

One afternoon after class, the teaching assistant came up to me and said a bunch of kids from class were getting together at his place for dinner. "You should come," he said.

"Sure. Why not?"

Well … when I showed up, it wasn't "a bunch of kids." It was just me and him. In his apartment. No crowd. No dinner party.

I awkwardly thanked him and made a quick exit. And unsurprisingly, I didn't do so well in that class.

For years afterward, I didn't think much about public speaking; in fact, I hadn't thought about that story in forever, until I started writing this book.

Because here I am, years later, standing on stages, telling stories for a living.

My journey into speaking started through volunteer work, where I was asked to share my story. I remember thinking, *What story? This is just … my life. Nothing special. Nothing anyone else would care about.* That was my mindset back then.

But the first time I stood on a stage and actually shared from my heart—something happened.

People laughed. People cried.

(Thankfully, not for the wrong reasons.)

They connected. And that's when it hit me: Storytelling moves people. It changes us. It brings us closer.

And here's the part that still stays with me today: We all have stories worth sharing … even if we've convinced ourselves otherwise.

YOUR STORIES ARE INSPIRING

I'm certain I'm not the only one who's ever felt like they live a simple, ordinary life with nothing particularly special to share. Maybe you've thought that too—that your life is just … *your life*, that nothing you've done could possibly make an impact on someone else. That couldn't be further from the truth.

Like me, you may need to let go of that limited mindset.

Sharing your story has the power to change lives. It can spark inspiration. It can help someone see the world in a whole new way. Most of all, sharing stories connects us, heart to heart.

When we open up about what we've been through and who we are, we create real space for healing and growth—not just for others, but for ourselves. The story you're afraid to share might be the one someone else needs to hear most.

The story you're afraid to share might be the one someone else needs to hear most.

The first time I stood on a stage and shared my story about John, my abusive high school boyfriend, I didn't expect it to be a big deal.

I was wrong.

It was the first time I had ever said those words out loud in front of a group. And two things happened.

First, I was caught off guard by just how emotional it felt. My mind even went blank for a second. I had never spoken that part of my story out loud before, and it hit me harder than I expected. Standing there, I realized I had an entire audience watching me share this story that I had felt so much shame for. Right then, I realized something I should've known all along: I had nothing to be ashamed of. What happened wasn't my fault. I didn't deserve it, and it was time to let that shame go.

In that moment, something shifted. The weight I'd been carrying began to lift. The limits I had placed on myself started to fade, and in their place, confidence continued to take root—REAL confidence, built from the inside out.

The second thing that happened was that, after I walked off the stage, woman after woman came up to me. They said things like, "I had a John too." Some had been through it themselves. Others had daughters in relationships like the one I'd just described.

Their words stayed with me, not only because they were vulnerable but because they reminded me of something so important: We're not alone. We don't talk about abusive relationships nearly enough. In that moment, I realized how many women carry these stories quietly, waiting for someone else to speak first.

Suddenly, we weren't strangers; we were connected. That's what happens when we own our stories and share them. We give other people permission to own theirs.

And that might be the most powerful thing of all.

YOU HAVE A STORY TO SHARE

I once sat next to a woman after a leadership workshop who leaned in and said, "I loved hearing your stories, but I don't think I really have one myself."

I replied, "Tell me about a time you did something that scared you."

She paused for a moment, thinking. Then she said, "Well … last year, I applied for a promotion at work. I didn't think I'd get it.

I almost didn't even apply. But I hit submit at the very last minute. My hands were shaking. I felt like an imposter. I kept thinking, *Who do I think I am?*"

"And?" I asked, already knowing where this was going.

She smiled—kind of quietly—and said, "I got it. I've been leading a team ever since. Some days, I still feel like I have no idea what I'm doing, but I show up. I listen. I figure it out as I go."

I looked at her and said, "That's your story."

She laughed and said, "No, that's just work."

But it's not *just* work. That story—of self-doubt, of hesitation, of showing up anyway—is one that so many of us carry. It's the story of quiet courage. Of stepping forward without having all the answers. Of not letting fear win.

That's the thing about stories: They don't have to be dramatic to matter. They don't have to come with headlines or heartbreak or huge turning points. Some of the most powerful stories come from those everyday moments—the ones where we choose to show up, to speak up, to try. Ordinary moments become extraordinary when you have the courage to share them.

Ordinary moments become extraordinary when you have the courage to share them.

You have a story too. It's there, whether you've told it yet or not. And when you finally begin to speak it out loud, you'll realize it was never "ordinary" after all.

Some stories are harder to tell than others. The story I shared about my experience with John was hard, especially as I said it out loud in front of a group of strangers. However, the feedback I received afterward on how sharing that story impacted others in the audience was transformational.

It's not that I needed the feedback, but knowing that I impacted even one person by sharing that very personal experience made it all worth it to me. In that moment, the pain and hardship didn't disappear, but they took on new meaning because they made someone else feel less alone.

I have discovered that oftentimes, it's in sharing those personal and vulnerable stories that we finally find closure. Sharing my story about John gave me an additional layer of closure because it made me realize that what I went through could actually help people. It put a positive spin on a very negative experience, and instead of keeping it bottled up inside and feeling shame about it, I could use it as a tool to help myself and others.

Living a life without limits really is so much about letting go of the limitations we put on ourselves. When we can let go of those things that are holding us back, we can change the world by inspiring the people in it.

THE POWER OF THE UNPOLISHED STORY

In a world where social media lets us curate whatever impression we want, it's more important than ever that the stories we share are real.

We get so used to seeing only the shiny moments—the perfectly filtered photos, the smiling kids, the "just made this from scratch" dinner. Sometimes, without even realizing it, we feel like we have to keep up. We stage the moments. We filter the mess. We post the wins and quietly bury the losses.

But guess what? Everyone you follow who looks like they have it all together? They're human too. You don't know their story unless they share it. You don't know what they're carrying behind that one happy snapshot.

A single photo says almost nothing about a person. It doesn't show the tears they shed on the bathroom floor, the job they didn't get, the argument they had that morning, or the weight of anxiety they carry silently through their day.

We don't often post about those moments. But those are the moments that make us real. They're the parts of our stories that connect us, ground us, and remind others that they're not alone. The messy parts of your story are where the real connection lives.

The messy parts of your story are where the real connection lives.

We all have moments like these. Let me say that again—we *all* have moments like these.

When we choose to share them honestly, that's where the real power is. That's where connection begins. That's when someone else feels a little less alone in their own mess.

Your story doesn't have to be perfect. It just has to be true.

TELLING HARD STORIES

You might be thinking, *I have a story, but it's too painful to share.*

I get that. I've been there.

It's like Maya Angelou said, "There is no greater agony than bearing an untold story inside you."[69]

That quote has always stuck with me because it is so very true. Holding on to a painful experience without ever speaking it out loud can feel like carrying a weight that never lightens. It sits in your chest. It creeps into your thoughts. And often, it hurts more to keep it in than it would to let it out.

I've learned that telling your story, especially the hard parts, is at least as much about helping yourself as it is about helping others. It's about helping *you.* Because when we don't speak our truth, our minds have a way of looping back to the past, forcing us to relive it again and again.

That's why telling your story out loud—whether it's to a friend, a therapist, or a trusted partner—can be such a powerful release. It doesn't erase the pain, but it gives it air. It gives *you* air. Telling your truth won't erase your pain, but it will lighten its weight.

Telling your truth won't erase your pain, but it will lighten its weight.

I kept parts of my story quiet for years. Sometimes it was due to shame. Sometimes fear. Sometimes I just didn't have the words. But I've learned that silence can be heavier than truth. Every time I've shared a part of my story, I've felt lighter, stronger, and more grounded in who I am.

When I finally told my story about John, it didn't just help me heal; it helped others feel seen. That's the beauty of sharing. You never know who needs to hear what you've lived through. You never know who's sitting in silence, thinking they're the only one.

You don't have to share your story with the whole world. Just start with someone safe. Someone who sees you. Someone who can hold space for you without judgment.

SEEK OUT THE STORIES OF OTHERS

If you haven't figured it out by now, I love stories.

Why? Because stories connect us. They build empathy, create understanding, and help us remember things in a way that facts and figures just can't. They show us what it looks like to live with courage, to overcome, to keep going when things get hard. Stories remind us that we're not alone—and that others have been where we are.

Think about the last speaker you heard. Do you remember their *stats*, or do you remember their *stories*?

We don't usually hang on to numbers for very long. They come and go. But stories stay with us. Researchers looked at more than 33,000 people and found that stories were remembered much more clearly and consistently than plain information.[70]

Yes, I know I just gave you a stat to prove my point—don't worry, you'll remember the story part. That's the beauty of it. Stories stick. That's why it's so important not just to share your story but to be curious about the stories of others. They're all around us if we're willing to ask and listen.

One of my favorite things to do when I travel is collect stories. Whether I'm sitting next to someone on a plane or riding in an Uber, I love learning about where people come from, what brought them here, and what matters most to them.

For example, once when I was in Washington, D.C., I noticed the Amharic script in my Uber driver's car. I asked where he was from, and when he said Ethiopia, we immediately had a connection—two of my children are from Ethiopia. From there, the conversation unfolded: his journey to the U.S., the family he had to leave behind, the conflict in Tigray, the loved ones he lost.

But what stayed with me the most wasn't just his story. It was his perspective. His deep gratitude—for life, for safety, for being here. He radiated hope, and I felt honored that he shared it with me.

I've had countless moments like that. Conversations that stay with me far longer than the trip itself, people whose names I may never know, but whose stories I'll never forget.

My kids know me too well. Anytime I strike up a conversation in an airport line, they exchange an eye roll and one of them says, "Here we go—Mom's about to get someone's full autobiography." And sure enough, I usually do.

Don't miss the chance to ask someone about their story. You never know what you'll learn or how it might change you. And sometimes, hearing someone else's story gives you the courage to finally share your own.

Because storytelling doesn't just bring us closer to each other. It brings us closer to ourselves.

YOUR STORY IS WHAT MAKES YOU UNIQUE

For generations, storytelling has been the way we have passed things down, such as our traditions, values, lessons, and history. It was how people remembered where they came from and how they helped others understand it too.

No two stories were ever exactly the same. They were shaped by place, time, and the people living through it all. That hasn't changed. Sure, we've swapped front porches and firepits for podcasts and Instagram posts, but at the core, storytelling still does what it's always done: It reminds us who we are, where we've been, and how far we've come.

Your story is unique; it's unlike anyone else's. No one has lived your exact life, seen the world through your eyes, or walked your exact path. That's what makes it powerful. That's what makes it yours. When you begin to embrace that truth—when you stop editing or shrinking or hiding the parts you think aren't "good enough"—you take a massive step toward REAL confidence.

As I've said several times, confidence doesn't come from perfection. It comes from honesty. It comes from ownership. Your story has made you who you are—the highs, the lows, the wins, and the missteps. All of it.

But here's the problem: We're so quick to hide the messy parts. We hold back the pieces we're scared people won't like. We soften the edges so we don't seem too complicated. We wrap our experiences in neat little bows so no one has to feel uncomfortable. But connection lives in those messy parts. That's where the courage is. That's where people see themselves in you. When you act like everything is perfect, you unintentionally make others feel like they're failing. But when you show up as your full self—bumps, bruises, beautiful truth and all—you give others permission to do the same.

So, here's my invitation to you: Start sharing your story. The whole thing. Not just the highlights. Not just the parts you've already made peace with. All of it. Because when you own your story, you free yourself. And when you share it, you make space for others to step into their own truth too. That's how we change the world—not by being perfect but by being real.

When you look in the mirror and see someone who's not afraid to be who they are, that's when confidence becomes real. Not from pretending, but from showing up fully and authentically.

KEEPING IT REAL

OWN YOUR STORY

Take a few minutes with a journal—or just a quiet moment to have a conversation with yourself—and answer these questions honestly. No filters. No edits. Just you.

1. **What's one part of your story you usually leave out when you introduce yourself?**

   Maybe it feels too messy, too painful, or too personal. Write it down anyway.

   ____

   ____

   ____

2. **Why do you think you hide that part?**

   Be kind here. This is about awareness, not judgment.

   ____

   ____

   ____

3. **What would it feel like to embrace that part instead of avoiding it?**

   Imagine telling your story without skipping it. What shifts?

   ____
   ____
   ____

4. **What's one thing you've learned from that experience that someone else might need to hear?**

   Chances are, your story could be someone else's survival guide.

   ____
   ____
   ____

5. **What's one small way you can start showing up more fully this week online, in a conversation, or even just with yourself?**

   You don't have to share everything. But you can start.

   ____
   ____
   ____

Chapter Fourteen

TRANSFORMATION

"I am no longer accepting the things I cannot change. I am changing the things I cannot accept."

ANGELA DAVIS

This is the chapter where we take everything we've learned about confidence and put it all together. The goal is *transformation*: letting go of self-doubt and becoming someone who lives with REAL confidence. Every mindset shift. Every Mirror Moment. Every time you choose courage over comfort and keep showing up, even when it's hard. This is the part of the journey where confidence becomes more than something you practice—it becomes part of who you are. And sometimes, the most powerful transformations don't happen all at once. They build slowly, quietly, in places you never expected. For me, one of those places was a podcast.

When we launched the *Her Unshakeable Confidence* podcast, my daughter, Olivia, was just twenty years old. And let's be honest, how many twenty-year-olds want to start a podcast with their mom? Somehow, she said yes. I thought we were starting a show to help others, to share lessons and stories about confidence. But somewhere along the way, the conversations started changing us too.

Each episode became a mirror. I heard my own growth in the questions I asked. I watched Olivia step more fully into her voice, no longer the quiet observer but a confident, thoughtful cohost who challenged me in the best ways. We were not just *talking about* transformation. We were *living* it.

Not all of it happened on the mic. Some of the biggest shifts happened behind the scenes, while walking the dogs, unloading the dishwasher, or in the quiet in-between moments when something from an episode stuck with us and kept unfolding.

We've had conversations that opened our eyes in new ways, about identity, motherhood, fear, and power. And the beauty of it all? The growth was never forced. It happened gradually, one honest reflection at a time.

This podcast was not just a project. It was a practice. A reminder to keep learning, keep showing up, and keep becoming, together.

That experience of growing through honest conversations, showing up even when it was uncomfortable, and reflecting on who we were becoming showed me what transformation really looks like. It is not instant. It is not perfect. But it is real. And that is what I want to walk you through next.

TRANSFORMATION FRAMEWORK

Real transformation happens when you stop spinning your wheels, step out of your own way, and finally start building momentum. Transformation doesn't start with a massive leap—it starts with one brave step.

Transformation doesn't start with a massive leap–it starts with one brave step.

I want to introduce you to the "Transformation Timeline Framework"—a road map for moving from self-limitation (aka, the mental quicksand most of us know too well) to full-blown self-confidence.

And I don't just mean the kind of confidence that *looks* good. I'm talking about the kind that actually *feels* good. The kind that lets you walk into a room, make decisions that align with your values, and live a life that's truly yours. That level of confidence may sound impossible, but all it really takes is a shift in how we see ourselves.

Because when *that* changes, everything else changes.

Let's break it down.

Stage 1: Self-Limitation–"I can't."

We all know this stage. It's the place where fear and self-doubt run the show, when you wake up already feeling behind. At this stage, you catch yourself thinking:

- I can't keep up.
- I'm not good enough.
- Why is everyone else crushing it while I'm just … here?

Here's how it shows up in real life:

- Hesitating to speak up because you're afraid of saying the wrong thing.
- Avoiding difficult conversations because they make your stomach flip.
- Second-guessing every decision, wondering if you're messing it all up.

Let's call it what it is: **fear.**

Fear of failing.

Fear of being judged.

Fear of not measuring up.

It's what keeps you stuck, playing small, and scrolling social media convincing yourself that *next week* you'll get it together. But let's be real—next week isn't the answer.

Here's the good news: This stage is just where we begin. It's not where we stay.

Stage 2: Self-Recognition—"I see my potential."

This is the "Wait a second … maybe I don't totally suck" stage. It's when you start noticing your own strength. You begin to think, *Hey … maybe I* can *do this.*

Here's how it shows up in real life:

- Celebrating small wins instead of brushing them off.
- Catching yourself saying, I've been through worse—I can handle this.
- Accepting a compliment instead of swatting it away with a nervous laugh.

You're starting to recognize that you bring something unique to the table—whether that's in your home, your friendships, your community, or your creative work.

Confidence grows every time you celebrate progress instead of perfection.

Confidence grows every time you celebrate progress instead of perfection.

It's like learning to ride a bike. You might wobble, but you're moving forward.

Keep pedaling.

Stage 3: Self-Realization—"I'm becoming who I'm meant to be."

Here's where things start to click. You're not just *noticing* your potential; you're *stepping into* it. You stop waiting for someone else to give you permission and start creating your own path.

Here's how it shows up in real life:

- Saying yes to something that excites you and scares you.
- Making confident decisions based on what feels right to you.
- Showing up fully—even if you don't have all the answers.

You start trusting yourself. You're not trying to prove your worth. Instead, you're *living it.* Stop waiting for permission to grow—your next chapter begins when you say yes to yourself.

That shift is where the real growth begins.

Stop waiting for permission to grow–your next chapter begins when you say yes to yourself.

Stage 4: Self-Confidence–"The world reflects my growth."

This is the turning point, the moment when what's happening *inside* you starts to shift what's happening *around* you. You walk through life with more clarity, more courage, and more calm.

Here's how it shows up in real life:

- You're making choices that align with your values, not your fears.
- Your relationships are stronger, healthier, and more honest.

- You've stopped settling, and you've started honoring what matters most.

You're not waiting for a perfect moment; rather, you're creating your life in real time. You've gone from playing small to showing up powerfully, and people notice. Doors open. That version of life you always wanted is no longer out of reach.

You're living it.

TRANSFORMING ONE STEP AT A TIME

So, how do we get there?

It's not about overnight transformation. Nobody wakes up one day and thinks, "Wow, I'm just so self-confident now!"

No, it's about small, intentional shifts—one step, one statement, one moment at a time.

We begin at Stage 1—Self-Limitation.

To progress to Stage 2—Self-Recognition, we use "I can" statements. These straightforward affirmations reshape your inner dialogue and create opportunities for growth and possibility. For example:

- I can say no without guilt.
- I can ask for help when I need it.
- I can delegate what doesn't need to be mine.
- I can press pause—and that's still progress.

Once we've reached Stage 2—Self-Recognition, the path to Stage 3—Self-Realization involves using "I see" statements.

These affirmations help you celebrate your achievements and link your efforts to meaningful results. For example:

- I see how far I've come.
- I see the positive impact I have on others.
- I see that my voice matters.
- I see the results of showing up with intention.

At this stage, it's time to embrace "I Am" statements to affirm your identity and strengths. These declarations anchor your growth and empower you to fully step into Stage 4—Self-Confidence, solidifying your transformation and owning your power. You might say:

- I am allowed to prioritize myself.
- I am aligned with my purpose and values.
- I am worthy of my goals and dreams.
- I am able to make time for what is important to me.

I get it—this might feel a little uncomfortable.

Maybe you're still side-eyeing the whole idea of affirmations, wondering how a few simple sentences could possibly shift something as deep as self-worth. Maybe part of you still hears that old voice saying, *It's not that easy.*

And you're right—transformation isn't easy. But it also isn't as impossible as we've been led to believe. Think about it: How many times have you said something harsh to yourself and believed it without question?

I'm not good enough.

I always mess things up.

Everyone else has it figured out but me.

If we can believe the negative things without proof, why wouldn't we at least *try* believing the good?

Affirmations are more than just words. They're daily reminders that you're allowed to speak to yourself with the same compassion you give everyone else. They interrupt the noise. They rewrite the story. And give your confidence a place to grow.

And if that still sounds too abstract—don't worry. There's science behind it.

Research shows affirmations aren't just feel-good fluff; they actually change the way your brain works. In fact, studies using fMRI scans show that repeating positive affirmations activates the brain's reward centers, the same areas triggered by things like chocolate or winning money.[71] They've also been shown to reduce stress, improve problem-solving under pressure, and build emotional resilience.

And here's where it gets even more interesting:

Self-confidence, which affirmations help build over time, has been directly linked to earning potential. One study found that people with higher confidence levels earn up to $28,000 more per year than those who struggle with self-doubt.[72]

So even if it feels a little awkward in the beginning, stick with it. You're not just saying nice things to yourself; you're literally training your brain to believe in your value.

And that belief is powerful.

MORNING MINDSET RESET

Too often we view transformation as some massive, immediate overhaul when, in reality, it's about small, intentional shifts—one step, one statement, one moment at a time.

"Fake it till you make it" doesn't produce real change. You know what does?

Saying it until you become it.

So, start your morning with a mindset reset by asking yourself, *What stage am I in today?* and then choosing the statements that will advance you into the next stage.

The goal is to do what you can to gradually move down the Transformation Timeline toward living without the pressure of limitations.

GO OUT THERE AND LIVE YOUR STORY

What will you choose today?

Will you let the pressure of the world keep you small?

Or will you rise—fully, boldly, and without apology?

Will you lead your life, not with fear, but with purpose and passion?

Because here's what I know: Your work is not small. Your choices are not insignificant. Every time you choose to show up as the highest version of yourself, you light the way for someone else.

Every step you take, every mountain you climb, every time you say, "I am enough," you're not just transforming yourself—you're transforming the world. Every time you rise, you remind others that they can rise too.

Every time you rise, you remind others that they can rise too.

You are the hero of this story.

You are the leader who inspires, the friend who uplifts, the parent who shows their children what's possible.

And together, with your courage and your commitment, you are building a legacy that will outlast you.

So, go. Be bold. Be brave. Be real.

The climb is steep, but the view is magnificent.

And the world is waiting for you to rise.

KEEPING IT REAL

YOUR AFFIRMATION ACTIVATION

You've just explored the power of self-talk and the stages of transformation. Now, let's put it into practice. We'll do that by choosing affirmations that resonate with you, rewriting the ones that don't, and making them yours.

Grab a journal or a piece of paper and take 5–10 minutes with these steps:

1. CHOOSE ONE "I CAN" STATEMENT

Which one speaks to where you are right now?

→ Write it down and finish this sentence:

When I say this, I feel ...

____

____

____

Now rewrite it in your own words if it helps the meaning land deeper.

____

____

____

2. CHOOSE ONE "I SEE" STATEMENT

Pick the one that feels like progress to you.

→ Now list 2–3 recent experiences that *prove it's true.*

____

____

____

Let yourself be proud. You've earned it.

3. CHOOSE ONE "I AM" STATEMENT

Say it out loud. Whisper it. Shout it in the car.

→ Then answer this:

What would change if I believed this every day?

____

____

____

4. WRITE YOUR OWN AFFIRMATION

Based on where you are in your story, create one new affirmation that fits your journey right now.

Start with:

- I can ...
- I see ...
- I am ...

Make it yours. Then put it somewhere you'll see it daily.

You don't need to believe it 100 percent yet. You just need to start. Every time you speak truth to yourself, you're building a new foundation—one that's real, strong, and completely yours.

____

____

____

PILLAR #4 EXERCISES

LIVE WITHOUT LIMITS

If you want to learn how to truly love the woman in the mirror, it's time to put your learning into practice. Here are ten different exercises to help build your confidence by loving the woman in the mirror. Choose one of these exercises and follow through with it. You can come back and choose a different exercise as often as you need to. Remember—when you change the way you see yourself, the world around you changes. So don't skip these exercises. They are an important part to building REAL confidence.

1. THE "I CAN" SHIFT

- **Write down five self-limiting beliefs that have been holding you back.**

  ____

  ____

  ____

  ____

  ____

- **Reframe each one into an empowering "I can" statement.**

  ____

  ____

- Read these new statements out loud each morning for a week.

2. THE BOLD ACTION CHALLENGE

- Choose one bold action you've been avoiding.

- Write down why this action is important for your growth.

- Set a deadline and take the action.

3. THE FEAR REFRAME

- Identify one fear that holds you back.

- Write down the worst-case scenario and the best-case scenario.

- Focus on taking one small step toward the best-case outcome.

4. THE "I AM" IDENTITY BUILDER

- Write down ten statements starting with "I am," focusing on positive traits or values.

- Review this list often and add to it as you grow.

5. SELF-PORTRAIT VISUALIZATION

- Close your eyes and picture yourself as the person you want to be.
- Visualize confidence, joy, and love radiating from within.
- Hold on to that image when self-doubt arises.

6. THE TRANSFORMATION TRACKER

- Each morning, ask yourself: "What stage am I in today?"
- Write down one step you can take to move to the next stage.

____

____

____

7. THE CONFIDENCE CONTRACT

- Write a short pledge to yourself about how you will step into your confidence.

____

____

____

- Sign and date it, then place it somewhere visible as a daily reminder.

8. CELEBRATE YOUR WINS WALL

- Dedicate a space in your home to display reminders of your achievements (certificates, photos, notes of encouragement).
- Each time you see it, take a moment to acknowledge your growth.

9. THE ENERGY AUDIT

- List five things that drain your energy and five things that fuel your confidence.

___
___
___
___
___
___
___
___
___
___

- Commit to reducing the negative influences and increasing the positive ones in your life.

10. THE POWER OF YOUR VOICE

- Each day, write down one situation where you spoke up, set a boundary, or expressed your opinion.

- At the end of the week, reflect on how using your voice changed your confidence.

Chapter Fifteen

GO CLIMB YOUR KILIMANJARO

"You must do the thing you think you cannot do."[73]

ELEANOR ROOSEVELT

Now that we've come to the end of the book, I want to take you back to the beginning by helping you visualize your own Kilimanjaro.

Remember how I said visualizing is an important part of seeing things differently? Let's put that into action. Picture yourself standing at the summit of a mountain. The air is crisp, the clouds are below you, and the world stretches out farther than you ever thought possible.

Your heart is pounding—but not from exhaustion. It's from pride, from that overwhelming feeling of accomplishment that comes from doing something really hard.

You did it. You made it to the top.

But this isn't just any mountain—it's your Kilimanjaro.

It's the goal you set, the challenge you faced, and the transformation you allowed yourself to go through.

The climb wasn't easy. Nothing worthwhile ever is.

In fact, it might have been the hardest thing you've ever done.

But every single step brought you here, to this moment.

You've arrived.

Can you see yourself standing there?

Can you feel the breeze? The clouds below your feet?

Can you feel the weight lift, the confidence settle in, and the satisfaction of reaching the summit?

Because if you can learn to see it—you can get there.

You can achieve it.

YOUR KILIMANJARO IS WAITING FOR YOU

Whatever brought you to this book, at this moment, wasn't a coincidence.

Your Kilimanjaro is waiting for you.

Maybe you already know what it is.

Maybe it's been whispering to you for years, quietly asking for your attention.

Or maybe it's something you've been avoiding because it feels too big, too hard, or too impossible.

Either way—you're here.

And you're ready to climb.

The REAL Method™ has given you the tools you need for the journey.

But the climb?

The climb is yours to make.

This is the moment you've been waiting for.

You didn't come this far to stop now.

As you put The REAL Method™ into action, every step you take will transform your life.

You'll stop scrolling through social media wishing for someone else's life—because you'll be living your own and loving it.

You'll stop worrying about what other people are doing—and start focusing on your own value, your own worth, and the good you're doing.

Most of all, you'll realize that by living your truth, you're not just changing *your* life—you're changing the world.

THE REAL METHOD™ REVIEW

Step One: Respect Yourself

Self-respect begins where self-sabotage ends.

Think back to how you spoke to yourself before you started this journey. How often did you criticize yourself? How often did you downplay your worth? How often did you shrink back from sharing your true self with others?

Respecting yourself means recognizing that your value doesn't depend on anyone else's opinion.

You are enough—right now, exactly as you are.

When you look in the mirror, respect the woman staring back at you. Honor her. Be kind to her with your words and your thoughts. And every single time you see your reflection, choose to believe in her.

Step Two: Embrace Your Failures

Your ability to grow comes from your willingness to try.

Think about a time you tried and didn't succeed. Maybe you felt embarrassed, disappointed, or frustrated. But what did you learn? What did it teach you about perseverance, courage, and grit?

Embracing failure is trusting that growth lives in the mess. It's falling down and deciding to stand back up with compassion. It's naming your strengths even when they feel hard to see. It's choosing to learn instead of giving up. It's reminding yourself that progress isn't perfect—it's movement, and you're still in it. And when you lead with your strengths, you build courage, confidence, and resilience.

It's also about choosing the right people to walk beside you—letting go of toxic relationships, and investing in those who lift you higher.

Failure doesn't get the final word.

You do.

Step Three: Ask Yourself What You Want

Discovering what you want creates space for who you're meant to be.

After reading this book, I hope you're starting to see what you want more clearly. I hope you're giving yourself permission to want what *you* want, not what other people expect from you.

It's easy to stay on autopilot. It's easy to do what's comfortable, what's familiar. But life is too short not to chase the things that light you up. Once you know what you want, calm your fears—and go for it.

Give yourself the time and grace to figure it out. Make self-care a priority, not an afterthought. And whatever you do, don't let anyone tell you that your dreams are too big.

Step Four: Live Without Limits

When you change the way you see yourself, the world around you changes.

Living without limits means remembering who you are when the world tells you to play small.

It's about daring to try even when you're unsure.

It's about facing your daily doubts—and choosing confidence anyway.

It's refusing to settle for "good enough" when you know you're made for more.

It's flipping the "I can't" into "I will."

The biggest limits you face are often the ones you create in your mind. When you live without limits, you realize you're far more capable, resilient, and powerful than you ever gave yourself credit for.

And finally, living without limits is about owning your story. Because your story matters. It's the thread that weaves us all together. So don't be afraid to share it. The world needs your voice.

CLAIMING YOUR SUMMIT

It's time to ask yourself:

What is my Kilimanjaro?

What's the mountain you want to climb?

Maybe it's setting boundaries in a relationship.

Maybe it's changing careers.

Maybe it's finally writing that book, or stepping outside your comfort zone to chase a dream you've carried for years.

Whatever it is, it matters.

Your Kilimanjaro is as unique as you are.

Your journey won't be perfect.

There will be days when you doubt yourself, when the climb feels too steep or the summit feels too far away.

But you are stronger than you think.

You've got this.

Keep moving forward.

Every step matters.

Every moment of progress brings you closer to the top.

And here's the good news:

You don't have to have it all figured out today.

Take the next step.

And then the next one.

And then the next.

That's how mountains are climbed—one step at a time.

When you reach the summit of your own Kilimanjaro, you'll experience the transformation that only comes from putting in the work to make it happen.

And in that moment, you'll see it:

You'll be the one smiling back at yourself in the mirror.

You'll be the one inspiring a stranger in an Uber.

You'll be the one pushing through doubts and chasing dreams, just like my mother did.

You'll be the one failing big—and rising even bigger—because you're not afraid to try.

And above all, you'll be the one living your dreams because you didn't just wish for them.

You worked for them. You believed in them. You believed in you.

IT'S TIME TO CLIMB

Looking up from the base of your Kilimanjaro might feel overwhelming. It might feel big, daunting, or downright impossible. That's okay. Just like every other journey you've started, every step you take—no matter how small—builds your courage, strengthens your confidence, and reminds you that you are capable of more than you think.

Believe me, I know what it feels like to stand at the bottom of a mountain that seems to stretch forever into the sky. That day in Tanzania, standing there at the base of Kilimanjaro, taught me something I'll never forget: Reaching the summit isn't about giant leaps or some sudden burst of strength—it's about steady, determined steps, taken one after another, even when you're tired, even when it's hard, even when the top still feels impossibly far away.

It's the same for you. You don't have to have everything figured out right now. You don't have to map out every twist and turn ahead of time. You just have to start. You have to keep moving forward, trusting that each step will lead you closer, even when it feels like you're standing still.

So here I am, inviting you to take that first step—to gather your courage, gather your confidence, and begin your climb.

Don't give up now. You have everything you need inside you. You have the clarity, the tools, and the strength you've been building all along. All that's left is to trust yourself enough to climb.

The mountain is waiting for you, and so is the version of yourself that's standing at the summit.

You are capable. You are worthy. You are ready. And I believe in you with every fiber of my being.

Now go climb your Kilimanjaro.

YOU.

ARE.

UNSHAKEABLE.

ACKNOWLEDGMENTS

To my family, thank you for being the steady foundation beneath every idea, every chapter, and every moment of doubt. Rob, your belief in me never wavered. Jacob, Emma, Olivia, Ari, Noah, Mili, and Abby, you brought laughter, honesty, and so much love into this process. You remind me why confidence, growth, and connection matter.

To my friends and community, thank you for your support, your encouragement, and the countless moments when you reminded me to keep going. Your presence in my life helped me move forward on the days when this journey felt heavy.

A special thank you to my publisher, Allison Trowbridge, whose steady guidance helped me reach parts of this story I might have overlooked on my own. Your insight, encouragement, and belief in the message of this book shaped every chapter in ways I will always appreciate.

To my editor and the entire publishing team, thank you for your care, your patience, and your attention to detail. You helped me bring clarity and strength to these pages.

Thank you to everyone who shared their experiences with me for this book. I am grateful for your openness.

To every woman who has ever questioned her worth or wondered if she was allowed to want more, this book is for you. Your courage is why I continue to write and speak. I hope these pages remind you of your own strength and help you see yourself with more kindness and truth.

And finally, to every reader who picked up this book, thank you. Thank you for trusting me with your time. My hope is that these words stay with you long after you close the pages.

Scan to access the reader guide, exercises, and other supporting resources.

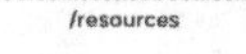

ENDNOTES

1 Maya Angelou, *Phenomenal Woman: Four Poems Celebrating Women* (Random House, 1995), 12.

2 Danielle Littlejohn, "What's Holding Women Back? Crises of Confidence in the Workplace," *Global Government Forum*, November 12, 2023, updated November 20, 2023, https://www.globalgovernmentforum.com/whats-holding-women-back-crises-of-confidence-in-the-workplace/.

3 Indeed Editorial Team, "Confidence at Work: Why Employers Should Nurture This Soft Skill," Indeed Lead Insights, January 23, 2020. https://www.indeed.com/lead/confidence-at-work.

4 Eleanor Roosevelt, *You Learn by Living: Eleven Keys for a More Fulfilling Life* (Harper & Brothers, 1960), 29.

5 Robert Tew, "Respect yourself enough to walk away from anything that no longer serves you, grows you, or makes you happy," Goodreads, accessed October 21, 2025, https://www.goodreads.com/quotes/7030921-respect-yourself-enough-to-walk-away-from-anything-that-no.

6 Aretha Franklin, "Respect," written by Otis Redding, recorded 1967, Atlantic Records.

7 Domestic Violence Intervention, Inc., "Teen Dating Violence," accessed September 19, 2025, https://www.dvifallon.org/resources/teen-dating-violence/.

8 Albert Bandura, "Self-Efficacy: Toward a Unifying Theory of Behavioral Change," *Psychological Review* 84, no. 2 (1977): 191–215, https://doi.org/10.1037/0033-295X.84.2.191.

9 Ulrich Orth, Richard W. Robins, and Kenneth F. Widaman, "Life-Span Development of Self-Esteem and Its Effects on Important Life Outcomes," *Journal of Personality and Social Psychology* 102, no. 6 (2012): 1271–1288, https://doi.org/10.1037/a0025558.

10 Confucius, *The Analects*, trans. Arthur Waley (Vintage Books, 1989), 61.

11 KPMG, *Advancing the Future of Women in Business: The KPMG Women's Leadership Study.* 2015.

12 Tara Sophia Mohr, "Why Women Don't Apply for Jobs Unless They're 100% Qualified," *Harvard Business Review*, August 25, 2014, https://www.hbr.org/2014/08/why-women-dont-apply-for-jobs-unless-theyre-100-qualified. Note: the Hewlett-Packard report referenced in the article is described as "internal," with no public data provided.

13 Oxford University Press, s.v. "Respect," in *Oxford English Dictionary*, accessed June 18, 2025, https://www.oed.com.

14 *OED*, s.v. "Respect."

15 Attributed to Judy Garland, quoted in *The Quotable Woman: The First 5,000 Years*, ed. Elaine Partnow (Facts on File, 1995), 278.

16 Junhyung Kim, Joon Hee Kwon, Joohan Kim, Eun Joo Kim, Hesun Erin Kim, Sunghyon Kyeong, and Jae Jin Kim, "The Effects of Positive or Negative Self-Talk on the Alteration of Brain Functional Connectivity by Performing Cognitive Tasks," *Scientific Reports* 11 (2021): 14873, https://doi.org/10.1038/s41598-021-94328-9.

17 People Management, "Exclusive: Seven in 10 Women Experience Imposter Syndrome at Work, Research Finds," *People Management*, April 23, 2019. https://www.peoplemanagement.co.uk/article/1919598/exclusive-seven-10-women-experience-imposter-syndrome-work-research-finds.

18 Sarah Biddlecombe, "Michelle Obama on living with imposter syndrome," *Stylist*, accessed September 20, 2025, https://www.stylist.co.uk/long-reads/michelle-obama-impostor-syndrome-career-advice-work-mental-health-relationships-becoming-book-us/240417.

19 Kristin Neff, "Self-Compassion: An Alternative Conceptualization of a Healthy Attitude Toward Oneself," *Self and Identity* 2, no. 2 (2003): 85–101, https://doi.org/10.1080/15298860309032.

20 Kristin D. Neff and Christopher K. Germer, "A Pilot Study and Randomized Controlled Trial of the Mindful Self-Compassion Program," *Journal of Clinical Psychology* 69, no. 1 (2013): 28–44, https://self-compassion.org/wp-content/uploads/publications/Neff-Germer-MSC-RCT-2012.pdf; Carol D. Ryff and Corey L. M. Keyes, "The Structure of Psychological Well-Being Revisited," *Journal of Personality and Social Psychology* 69, no. 4 (1995): 719–727, https://midus.wisc.edu/findings/pdfs/830.pdf; and Ed Diener, Shigehiro Oishi, and Richard E. Lucas, "Personality, Culture, and Subjective Well-Being: Emotional and Cognitive Evaluations of Life," *Annual Review of Psychol-*

ogy 54 (2003): 403–425, https://www.annualreviews.org/content/journals/psych/54/1.

21 Claudine Clucas, Philip J. Corr, Heather Wilkinson, and Astrid Schepman, "Appraisal Self-Respect: Scale Validation and Construct Implications," *Current Psychology* 42, no. 23 (2023): 19681–19698, https://doi.org/10.1007/s12144-022-03093-z; and Srini Pillay, MD, "Greater Self-Acceptance Improves Emotional Well-Being," *Harvard Health Publishing*, May 16, 2016, https://www.health.harvard.edu/blog/greater-self-acceptance-improves-emotional-well-201605169546.

22 Brené Brown, *Rising Strong: The Reckoning. The Rumble. The Revolution.* (Spiegel & Grau, 2015), 45.

23 Dove, *"Global State of Beauty Report"* (2024), accessed June 2024, https://www.dove.com/us/en/campaigns/purpose/global-state-of-beauty.html.

24 Courtney Kennedy and Arnold Lau, "Most Americans Believe in Intelligent Life Beyond Earth; Few See UFOs as a Major National Security Threat," Pew Research Center, June 30, 2021, https://www.pewresearch.org/religion/2021/06/30/most-americans-believe-in-intelligent-life-beyond-earth-few-see-ufos-as-a-major-national-security-threat/.

25 National Organization for Women, "Get the Facts: Body Image," *NOW Foundation*, accessed September 27, 2025, https://now.org/now-foundation/love-your-body/love-your-body-whats-it-all-about/get-the-facts/.

26 *Teen Health and the Media*, University of Washington, "Fast Facts: Body Image," accessed September 20, 2025, https://depts.washington.edu/thmedia/view.cgi?page=fastfacts§ion=bodyimage.

27 National Organization for Women, "Get the Facts: Body Image."

28 National Organization for Women Foundation, "Get the Facts: Love Your Body," accessed June 18, 2025, https://now.org/now-foundation/love-your-body/love-your-body-whats-it-all-about/get-the-facts/.

29 Women's Confidence Report 2021, "American women seek external validation to boost their Confidence," Alison Shamir, October 18, 2021, https://alisonshamir.com/2021-womens-confidence-report/.

30 Anne Craig, "The Discovery of Thought Worms Opens a Window on the Mind," *Queen's Gazette*, July 1, 2020, https://www.queensu.ca/gazette/stories/discovery-thought-worms-opens-window-mind.

31 Fred Luskin, *Forgive for Good: A Proven Prescription for Health and Happiness* (HarperOne, 2003).

32 Christopher N. Cascio et al., "Self-Affirmation Activates Brain Systems Associated with Self-Related Processing and Reward and Is Reinforced by Future Orientation," *Social Cognitive and Affective Neuroscience* 11, no. 4 (2016): 621–629, https://doi.org/10.1093/scan/nsv136.

33 Norman Doidge, *The Brain That Changes Itself: Stories of Personal Triumph from the Frontiers of Brain Science* (Penguin Life, 2007).

34 Masayuki Tsujimoto, Toshiki Saito, Yutaka Matsuzaki, et al., "Role of Positive and Negative Emotion Regulation in Wellbeing and Health: The Interplay between Positive and Negative Emotion Regulation Abilities Is Linked to Mental and Physical Health," *Journal of Happiness Studies* 25 (2024), https://doi.org/10.1007/s10902-024-00714-1.

35 David R. Hamilton, "The Science of Affirmations," *DrDavidHamilton.com*, accessed September 21, 2025, https://drdavidhamilton.com/the-science-of-affirmations/.

36 David Tod, James Hardy, and Emily Oliver, "Effects of Self-Talk: A Systematic Review," *Journal of Sport and Exercise Psychology* 33, no. 5 (2011): 666–687, https://doi.org/10.1123/jsep.33.5.666.

37 Alyssa Bailey, "Suni Lee Gave a Powerful Speech About Letting Go of Fear at the Apex for Youth Gala," *Elle*, April 11, 2025, https://www.elle.com/culture/celebrities/a64456169/suni-lee-apex-for-youth-gala-speech-2025

38 Emma Burleigh, "Simone Biles Shares Her Advice for New Graduates Who Feel Overwhelmed or Doubt Themselves," *Fortune*, May 15, 2025, https://fortune.com/2025/05/15/simone-biles-advice-new-graduates-overwhelm-doubt/.

39 Malissa Rodenburg, "Valarie Allman Used Mantras to Win Gold. Here's How You Can Too," Women's Running, August 9, 2021, https://www.womensrunning.com/culture/news/valarie-allman-olympics-gold-mantras/.

40 Kathryn Lindsay, "Jennifer Lopez's Daily Affirmations Are Going to Fix My Life," *Refinery29*, March 15, 2018, https://www.refinery29.com/en-us/2018/03/193692/jennifer-lopez-bazaar-cover-interview.

41 Megan Decker, "Alicia Keys Says This Is Her Biggest Tip for Glowing Skin," *Refinery29,* June 8, 2021, accessed June 2025, https://www.refinery29.com/en-us/2021/04/10396327/alicia-keys-biggest-tip-glowing-skin.

42 Maya Angelou, *Letter to My Daughter* (Random House, 2009), 28.

43 Aumyo Hassan and Sarah J. Barber, "The Effects of Repetition Frequency on the Illusory Truth Effect," *Cognitive Research: Principles and Implications* 6, Article 38 (2021), https://doi.org/10.1186/s41235-021-00301-5.

44 John M. Gottman and Robert W. Levenson, "What Predicts Change in Marital Interaction Over Time? A Study of Alternative Models," *Family Process* 38, no. 2 (1999): 143–158, https://doi.org/10.1111/j.1545-5300.1999.00143.x; see also The Gottman Institute, "The Magic Relationship Ratio, According to Science," accessed September 21, 2025, https://www.gottman.com/blog/the-magic-relationship-ratio-according-science/.

45 Zig Ziglar, "It's not how far you fall, but how high you bounce that counts," Ziglar.com, accessed October 21, 2025, https://www.ziglar.com/quotes/its-not-how-far-you-fall/.

46 Kathleen Elkins, "Spanx Founder Sara Blakely: My Dad Encouraged Me to Fail," *Business Insider*, October 26, 2016, https://www.businessinsider.com/spanx-founder-sara-blakely-redefine-failure-2016-10.

47 Elkins, "Spanx Founder Sara Blakely."

48 Elkins, "Spanx Founder Sara Blakely."

49 Simone Knego, *The Extraordinary UnOrdinary You: Follow Your Own Path, Discover Your Own Journey* (Lioncrest Publishing, 2020).

50 Shonda Rhimes, *Year of Yes: How to Dance It Out, Stand in the Sun and Be Your Own Person* (Simon & Schuster, 2015), 311.

51 Steve Maraboli, *Unapologetically You: Reflections on Life and the Human Experience* (A Better Today Publishing, 2013), 22.

52 Naz Beheshti, "Toxic Influence: An Average Of 80% Of Americans Have Experienced Emotional Abuse," *Forbes*, May 15, 2020, https://www.forbes.com/sites/nazbeheshti/2020/05/15/an-average-of-80-of-americans-have-experienced-emotional-abuse/.

53 Institute for Women's Policy Research, "Dreams Deferred: A Survey on the Impact of Intimate Partner Violence on Survivors' Education, Careers, and Economic Security," IWPR Publication No. D475 (Washington, DC: Institute for Women's Policy Research, 2020), 4, https://iwpr.org/wp-content/uploads/2020/09/C475_IWPR-Report-Dreams-Deferred.pdf.

54 Vincent van Gogh, *The Letters of Vincent van Gogh*, ed. Ronald de Leeuw (Penguin Classics, 1997), Letter 155 to Theo van Gogh, 1879.

55 Rhonda Byrne, *The Secret* (Atria Books, 2006).

56 "Fastest row of the Mid-Pacific east to west by a team of three (female)," *Guinness World Records*, accessed September 27, 2025, https://www.guinnessworldrecords.com/world-records/704017-fastest-open-class-row-of-the-mid-pacific-east-to-west-by-a-team-of-three-female.

57 "Rob's 10K Friends," *Rob Lawless*, accessed September 27, 2025, https://www.robs10kfriends.com/.

58 Oprah Winfrey, *O, The Oprah Magazine*, May 2000.

59 Rethink Mental Illness, "'Stigma Effect' Stops Three in Five People Experiencing Mental Illness from Seeking Help, Survey Reveals," Rethink Mental Illness, May 15, 2023. https://www.rethink.org/news-and-stories/media-centre/2023/05/stigma-effect-stops-three-in-five-people-experiencing-mental-illness-from-seeking-help-survey-reveals/.

60 Katie Reed, quoted in *The Good Trade*, "50 Self-Care Quotes to Inspire You," accessed September 21, 2025, https://www.thegood-trade.com/features/s

61 Mental Health First Aid USA, "6 Steps to Turn Your Self-Care Strategies into a Routine," *Mental Health First Aid*, March 14, 2022, https://www.mentalhealthfirstaid.org/2022/03/how-and-why-to-practice-self-care/.

62 Vincent van Gogh, quoted in *The Letters of Vincent van Gogh*, ed. Theo van Gogh (New York Graphic Society, 1958).

63 Christopher M. Whaley, et al., "Female Physicians Earn An Estimated $2 Million Less Than Male Physicians Over A Simulated 40-Year Career," *Health Affairs* 40, no. 11 (2021), https://doi.org/10.1377/hlthaff.2021.00461.

64 U.S. Census Bureau, *Income and Poverty in the United States: 2022*, Report No. P60-279 (Washington, DC: U.S. Government Printing Office, 2023).

65 Brianna Wiest, *101 Essays That Will Change the Way You Think* (CreateSpace Independent Publishing Platform, 2016).

66 Michael Hyatt, *Free to Focus: A Total Productivity System to Achieve More by Doing Less* (Baker Books, 2019).

67 Ivana Greco, "Are Tradwives Part of Our Past or Our Future—or Neither?" *Institute for Family Studies Blog*, April 7, 2025, https://ifstudies.org/blog/are-tradwives-part-of-our-past-or-our-future-or-neither.

68 Brené Brown, *The Gifts of Imperfection: Let Go of Who You Think You're Supposed to Be and Embrace Who You Are* (Hazelden, 2010), 23.

69 Maya Angelou, *I Know Why the Caged Bird Sings* (Random House, 1969), 192.

70 Jingyuan Li, Anh T. P. Nguyen, Cindy P. Ta, et al., "Memory and Comprehension of Narrative Versus Expository Texts: A Meta-Analysis," *Psychonomic Bulletin & Review* 28, no. 3 (2021): 732–749, https://doi.org/10.3758/s13423-020-01853-1.

71 Christopher N. Cascio, et al., "Self-Affirmation Activates Brain Systems Associated with Self-Related Processing and Reward and Is Reinforced by Future Orientation," *Social Cognitive and Affective Neuroscience* 11, no. 4 (2016): 621–29, https://doi.org/10.1093/scan/nsv136.

72 Timothy A. Judge and Charlice Hurst, "Capitalizing on One's Advantages: Role of Core Self-Evaluations in Interpersonal Success," *Journal of Applied Psychology* 92, no. 5 (2007): 1212–27, https://doi.org/10.1037/0021-9010.92.5.1212.

73 Eleanor Roosevelt, *You Learn by Living: Eleven Keys for a More Fulfilling Life* (Harper & Brothers, 1960), 29.